DESIGNING WITH

CLIMBERS

THE JOY OF GARDENING

DESIGNING WITH

CLIMBERS

BY RICHARD ROSENFELD
PHOTOGRAPHS BY JERRY HARPUR AND MARCUS HARPUR

COURAGE
BOOKS

AN IMPRINT OF RUNNING PRESS
PHILADELPHIA · LONDON

Senior designer	Ashley Western
Senior editor	Annabel Morgan
Editors	Polly Boyd,
	Jane Chapman,
	Samantha Gray
Picture research	Mel Watson,
	Kate Brunt
Production controller	Patricia Harrington
Publishing director	Anne Ryland

Printed and bound in China

Library of Congress Cataloging-in-Publication number
98–72367

ISBN 0-7624-0471-X

This edition published in the
United States in 1999 by
Courage Books, an imprint of
Running Press Book Publishers
125 South Twenty-second Street
Philadelphia, Pennsylvania
19103-4399

Visit us on the web!
www.runningpress.com

CONTENTS

Introduction

Climbing plants are tremendously versatile. They bring a strong vertical element to planting schemes, and add color and interest without taking up valuable ground space. Alternatively, some are suitable for ground cover. Climbers are invaluable for their ability to disguise unsightly features—for example, an unattractive fence, shed, or tree stump—and to soften bleak building materials, such as concrete or new bricks. They also serve to provide privacy, shade, and shelter in gardens in exposed or built-up areas. Above all, climbers are highly ornamental. Many are strong in architectural form, while others produce colorful flowers and berries or striking foliage.

How climbers climb

Climbing plants can be loosely divided into five different types: scrambling climbers; twining climbers; tendril climbers; aerial root climbers; and thorny roses.

Scrambling climbers, like some jasmines or *Bougainvillea*, have flexible stems that, in the wild, nose through and grow over other shrubs and trees. They have no means of supporting themselves, so they need to be tied to a trellis or wire framework if they are not to clamber over other plants.

Twining climbers, such as wisterias, twist their stems around their supports. Some twine clockwise (such as the Japanese *Wisteria floribunda*), some counterclockwise (like the Chinese *Wisteria sinensis*). All twiners need some type of permanent support, such as a trellis or wire; alternatively, they can be grown through trees and shrubs.

Some climbers climb using tendrils, which shoot out and coil around their support. A tendril may be a modified leaf stalk, as in the case of clematis, or stem, as in *Passiflora*. Some tendril climbers—Virginia creeper (*Parthenocissus quinquefolia*), for example—cling by means of adhesive pads at the tendril tips,

Right: *Bougainvillea* × *buttiana* 'Mrs Butt' will grow readily in the summer garden, creating a splash of intense color, but over winter the plant needs a cool, frost-free conservatory.

which lock on to the nearest surface. The latter require no support, except during the early stages, when they will need the help of stakes or wire to guide the plant in the right direction, until it is able to establish contact with its intended support.

Also needing no support are the aerial root climbers, such as ivies (*Hedera*). These produce tiny hairs, or aerial roots, along the stem, and have adhesive pads at the tips that glue themselves to supports like tree trunks, branches, and boulders. With tropical plants, such as *Philodendron*, the aerial roots also latch onto neighboring plants. The fifth and final group includes those roses with thorns, which anchor themselves as they spread.

Supports

Climbers are usually grown against walls or fences, but there are many other more inventive, quirky ways to grow them: send them up brightly painted poles, antique lamp posts, or pillars. Look around architectural salvage yards and scrap yards for strange twisted metal spires. Use ropes, lattice frames, pergolas, trees, a pillar of arched loops, willow frames or wigwams (*see page 74*)— the choice is vast. Several companies make ready-made iron structures for climbers. If they don't have what you are looking for, you could commission a blacksmith to make something to your specification. Deciduous climbers need attractive supports as the supports are on view during winter months.

Above: **A typical garden of about 100 x 40 ft (30 x 12 m) does not mean that you have only 4,000 sq ft (360 sq m). There is lots of space above ground for some first-rate climbers. Here, colorful sweet peas are seen against a background of violet-flowered *Solanum crispum* 'Glasnevin' and roses.**

Right: **The hop, *Humulus lupulus* 'Aureus', combines well with a scented rose and a honeysuckle, adding light green foliage to the mixed planting. The hop can grow 20 ft (6 m) in a summer, and is ideal for scrambling over fences and trellis, perhaps acting as a screen to create privacy from neighbors.**

Numerous climbing plants grow happily against the house wall: try vigorous growers like *Hydrangea petiolaris*, which can reach 40 ft (12 m), and *Jasminum officinale*, charging up the drainpipe. Many climbers are suitable for growing in pots in solaria, such as the tender *Bougainvillea* and the Paraguayan *Solanum rantonnetii*; both may be brought outdoors in the summer.

Growing climbers

There is a host of stunning climbing plants to choose from: some flower prolifically (*Rosa* 'Parkdirektor Riggers'), while others flower just for a few days or have a single burst in summer (*Rosa* 'Paul's Himalayan Musk'). There are those that provide spectacular autumn leaf color, such as *Vitis vinifera*, or fragrant blooms, like jasmine.

When selecting climbers, make sure they are suitable for the site. Some are fairly tender and require the shelter of a warm wall in cool climates (*Trachelospermum jasminoides*); there are many hardy climbers, however, such as ivies, that survive happily without any protection at all. Many climbers need full sun (*Cobaea scandens*), while several tolerate shade (*Hedera helix*). For year-round cover or privacy, choose evergreen climbers such as ivies.

The weight of the climber, climbing method, and rate of growth are also important considerations. Some climbers, such as the *Tropaeolum* species, are slimline whippets and can be grown against almost any support. However, there are many that are extremely heavy, like *Hydrangea petiolaris*, and these need a strong supporting structure to bear their weight.

You also need to be aware that some climbers can cause damage in certain situations: wisterias can easily climb onto a roof and dislodge loose slates; the adhesive aerial root pads of a thick-stemmed, unpruned ivy can damage cement mortar; and the adhesive tendril tips of Virginia creeper can ruin paintwork. In addition, some climbers are extremely vigorous: *Rosa filipes* 'Kiftsgate', for example, can spread up to 100 ft (30 m).

All gardens benefit from a good selection of ornamental climbers, but in a small garden, they are vital. There might be no more room on the ground for plants, but high up, there is plenty.

The heights of the climbers that are listed in this book are approximate, as growth will depend on the aspect, soil, climate, and the plant's vigor. Fully hardy means plants can survive to 5°F (−15°C), frost hardy to 23°F (−5°C), half hardy to 32°F (0°C), and frost tender indicates plants that may not survive at temperatures that fall below 41°F (5°C).

Top left: ***Hedera helix*** **'Green Ripple' is an excellent, all-purpose ivy. A quick sprinter, it grows 6 ft (2 m) high, and has large leaves. It is ideal for covering uninteresting walls or fences. You can even grow it as evergreen ground cover.**

Above: **The ultimate powerhouse rose for fast growth, *Rosa filipes* 'Kiftsgate' can reach up to 100 ft (30 m).**

Many climbers provide delicious scents that can be enjoyed outside—on a balmy summer's evening—or inside, through an open door or window. Fragrant climbers are best planted in a sheltered, warm site: the more enclosed the space, the more powerful the flowers' perfume will be.

SCENTED

Clematis

One of the earliest of the fragrant climbers is the mid-spring flowering *Clematis armandii* (*Group 1, see page 76*). It has evergreen foliage, bronze when young, and swags of delightful white flowers exuding scents of almond mixed with vanilla. *C. a.* 'Apple Blossom' is also an excellent climber, with white flowers tinged pink. Both need a sheltered, sunny wall where the buds can develop, and new growth will not get killed by frost. They can grow easily to 20 ft (6 m), and look good trained along the ridge of a long, low wall, with the scent about face high. If left alone, they will form a mounding thicket.

The vanilla-scented *Clematis montana* and its cultivars (*Group 1, see page 76*) have plenty of verve and vigor. They flower later, mostly in late spring to early summer, and produce flowers for about four weeks in mauves, pinks, and white. Many reach 25 ft (8 m) or more, and can shoot up a hedge or tree

Above: ***Clematis armandii* is an early-flowering clematis with long, slim, glossy evergreen leaves and a gorgeous, rich spring scent.**

Right: **A rampant *Clematis montana* demands a companion with vigor, such as this scented honeysuckle.**

Opposite page, left: ***Clematis rehderiana* was introduced to Britain by the great plant hunter "Chinese" Wilson in 1908. The flowers have the soft scent of cowslips.**

Opposite page, right: **Probably the hardiest montana is *Clematis m.* f. *grandiflora*. It can reach as high as 35 ft (11 m) and has white flowers set against dark foliage.**

Train *Clematis armandii* along the ridge of a low wall to best appreciate the almond-vanilla scent of the flowers.

(avoid apple trees, which are pink with blossom at the same time). They are also excellent for blotting out garden eyesores, such as new sheds; bear in mind, however, that they are deciduous, so will not offer year-round concealment. *C. m.* 'Mayleen', *C. m.* 'Pink Perfection', and *C. m.* 'Elizabeth' are all pink, the latter having the strongest scent and turning whitish in shade. *C. m.* 'Picton's Variety' (deep pink) and *C. m.* 'Broughton Star' (pink) are better for smaller gardens, growing to a more manageable height of 15 ft (5 m).

The pick of the summer clematis begins with the early summer, pale pink *Clematis* 'Fair Rosamond' (*Group 2, see page 76*). It only reaches 6½ ft (2 m) high, but has a delicious whiff of violets. Flowering simultaneously, or slightly later, is *C. montana* var. *wilsonii* (*Group 1, see page 76*), which blooms from mid- to late summer. It grows 25 ft (8 m) high, and some cultivars have a strong scent of hot chocolate. The yellow-flowered *C. rehderiana* (*Group 3, see page 76*), with downturned, bell-like flowers from

midsummer to mid-autumn, is also a vigorous, swarming climber, reaching 22 ft (7 m). Grow it up a wall or into a tree, so that you can peer up into its nodding flowers.

The final four clematis are all late-summer performers (*Group 3, see page 76*). The most strongly perfumed is *Clematis flammula*, which erupts in a great whoosh of white, almond-scented flowers that stand out beautifully against shiny, dark green leaves. Originally from the southern Mediterranean, it thrives in heat and fast-draining soil. It is excellent sprinting up trees and can reach 15 ft (5 m) high. Also flowering in late summer is *C. × triternata* 'Rubromarginata', with gorgeous red-edged white flowers that smell of hawthorn; at 12 ft (4 m) high, it can easily charge up a fence. The recently reintroduced *C. aethusifolia* is smaller, at 6½ ft (2 m), and produces pale yellow flowers with a lovely cowslip-daphne scent in late summer to early autumn. *C. serratifolia*, 10 ft (3 m) high, flowers for about four weeks and smells of lemon.

Wisterias

If you are looking for a big scented performer to clothe large areas in late spring and early summer, consider an oriental wisteria. There are approximately forty wisterias to choose from, which basically divide into two groups: *Wisteria sinensis* and *Wisteria floribunda*. Both are twining climbers: the former are Chinese, and coil counterclockwise; the latter Japanese, and coil clockwise. Wisterias come in a small choice of colors, mainly white, pinks, lilacs, and blues, and can reach 35 ft (11 m) easily.

The Chinese wisteria (*W. sinensis*) and its cultivars are much more vigorous than the Japanese types. The Chinese wisterias flower in late spring and often again in late summer, and have numerous larger, more scented flowers (*W. s.* 'Prolific' certainly lives up to its name). The flowers of *W. sinensis* are lilac, and *W. s.* 'Alba' has glorious white blooms. Avoid Chinese wisterias if your garden suffers from late spring frosts, or they will not produce any flowers.

One of the best Japanese wisterias is the two-toned, blue-violet *Wisteria floribunda* 'Multijuga', which bears the longest racemes, sometimes up to 3 ft (90 cm) long. One was even recorded as having racemes 6 ft (1.8 m) long. *W. f.* 'Alba' is white, and *W. f.* 'Peaches and Cream' is white with pink buds.

Left: **For the best wisteria scent, choose *Wisteria sinensis*. This will be a gamble in some regions as it flowers in late spring and the buds are susceptible to frost damage. In good years, however, you can have a superb display.**

Right: **Growing a high-performance wisteria on a wall or pergola means pruning it twice a year, in late summer and winter. If that is daunting, grow the wisteria into a sturdy tree to eliminate the need to prune.**

Wisterias create a stunning show in the garden with richly scented flowers and thick, decorative stems.

Opposite page, far left: **The wisteria for long racemes is *W. floribunda* 'Multijuga'. The flowers are displayed best by training the stems into large, looping and twisting shapes. When leafless, the stems provide a winter feature.**

Opposite page, left: **Mauve-flowered wisterias are incredibly popular, but the white-flowered types, like this *Wisteria floribunda* 'Alba', have their own pure, distinctive beauty and create a breathtaking show.**

Because wisterias have such richly scented flowers—albeit only for about two weeks—and massive stems, they deserve a prominent place in the garden. Grow them as standards, or tie them to pergolas or sunny house walls, sending pruned horizontal branches around windows. Alternatively, train two together to make an arch. Wisterias look good underplanted with tulips and forget-me-nots in spring, followed by alliums with their startling, large round heads, and columbines (*Aquilegia*) in near-black colors. *Wisteria sinensis* looks marvelous growing up a mature yew or hawthorn, with its flowers tumbling out of the host.

Most grafted wisterias—distinguished by the base of the stem being slightly darker than the upper wood—should flower in their third year, provided they experience hot, dry conditions the previous summer and are pruned correctly (*see page 77*). They are unlikely to flower prolifically for another year or two. Chinese wisterias may flower one year earlier than Japanese types. Avoid wisterias grown from seed—they can take twenty years to flower.

Honeysuckles

No garden should be without a scented honeysuckle. The most fragrant is *Lonicera japonica* 'Halliana', which flowers from early summer to autumn. It has a fruity scent and produces 30 ft (10 m) of thick, tangled growth. It scrambles happily through trees, and also makes an excellent screen, since it is virtually evergreen. To restrict growth and promote flowering, prune it in spring, cutting the old growth back hard at least every other year. The flowers are white fading to yellow, followed by blue-black berries. At its feet, plant the mauve *Nepeta sintenisii* 'Six Hills Giant': this has a large, full habit and reaches about 3 ft (90 cm) high.

Lonicera × *americana* is deciduous and slightly more modest, reaching 20 ft (6 m), with clove-scented yellow flowers and red berries. Tie it to a pillar, pole, or obelisk, and grow magenta *Geranium psilostemon* beneath. Alternatively, grow it against a shady wall with the small deciduous fern *Adiantum pedatum*.

Above: **A structured setting for an abundant display of the scented *Lonicera japonica* 'Halliana' is provided by the strap-shaped leaves of a phormium and a cordyline.**

Right: **_Lonicera periclymenum_ 'Belgica' is a superior form of the species hedgerow honeysuckle. It has a strong scent in midsummer. You could also try 'Serotina'.**

Roses

Roses are among the most beautiful of all flowering plants, and fill the garden with their sweet, voluptuous scents. There is a vast and diverse range for the gardener to choose from, including over sixty climbing and rambling roses.

Climbing roses have large flowers, produced singly or in clusters; most repeat flower all summer. Climbers are generally slightly more manageable than ramblers: they are ideal for walls and fences (grow them up and around a bedroom window), and can also be trained around pillars, and over bowers and arches. Climbers often have exposed bare stems near the ground. Prune regularly (*see page 77*), and use plants such as the purple perennial *Stachys byzantina*, 18 in (45 cm) high, or blue or white campanulas to provide cover around the stems.

There are five excellent red-flowered climbers. Even on light soils, *Rosa* 'Château de Clos-Vougeot, Climbing' can reach a height of 12 ft (4 m). It has a strong, deep scent, with some later flowers; *R.* 'Ena Harkness, Climbing' grows slightly taller, at 15 ft (5 m), with hanging heads you can peer up into and some later flowers. *R.* 'Etoile de Hollande, Climbing' has a fabulous rich scent, reaches 15 ft (5 m), and is recurrent. For a rich, dark purple-red color, try *R.* 'Guinée', 15 ft (5 m) high, setting it against a light

background for best effect. *R.* 'Crimson Glory, Climbing', 12 ft (4 m) high, is another excellent climber with large double, extremely fragrant dark red blooms.

Fewer excellent whites are available. There is the impressive whitish pink *Rosa* 'Madame Alfred Carrière', 15 ft (5 m) high, and the lemon-white *R.* 'Paul's Lemon Pillar', 15 ft (5 m) high, with a marvelous scent. *R.* 'Purity', 12 ft (4 m) high, has a strong scent but masses of prickles and few repeat flowers. *R.* 'Iceberg, Climbing' has a long flowering season, but is only 10 ft (3 m) high. The most vigorous climber is the notorious *R. filipes* 'Kiftsgate'. It can put on 20 ft (6 m) in a season and can reach as much as 100 ft (30 m). It needs time to get going, but gives good security and 18 in (45 cm) wide bunches of scented, creamy flowers.

The best scented climbing yellows include the first-rate buff-colored *Rosa* 'Gloire de Dijon', 15 ft (5 m) high, with a long flowering season; *R.* 'Golden Dawn, Climbing', 12 ft (4 m) high, with a delicious scent and sporadic later blooms; and *R.* 'Lady Hillingdon, Climbing', 15 ft (5 m) high, a richly scented beauty which has a long flowering season and tolerates light, free-draining soil. The 10 ft (3 m) high *R.* 'Maigold' has a glorious scent and some later flowers. Other good yellow climbers include *R.* 'Easlea's Golden Rambler', 12 ft (4 m) high; *R.* 'Lawrence Johnston', 25 ft (8 m) high; and *R.* 'Leverkusen', 10 ft (3 m) high.

Above left: **The bush *Rosa* 'Iceberg' may reach only 32 in (80 cm) in height, but there is also a climbing version, which was introduced in 1968. *R.* 'Iceberg, Climbing' grows 10 ft (3 m) high and has glossy leaves with an abundant display of flowers. Extremely reliable, it blooms throughout the summer.**

Above right: ***Rosa* 'Iceberg, Climbing' can also be grown as a standard rose, trained to form a white, head-high ball thick with massed white roses. This would make an eyecatching focal point in a more formal garden and is also ideal for enlivening the back of the perennial border.**

Climbing roses are ideal for covering walls and fences— if possible, grow a richly scented type up a house wall and train it around a bedroom window so that fragrance floods in when the window is open in summertime.

Finally, there are some excellent pink climbers. *Rosa* 'Madame Abel Chatenay, Climbing', 15 ft (5 m) high, is exquisite, with plentiful repeat flowers and a rich scent. *R.* 'New Dawn' reaches 5 ft (1.5 m) higher, with glossy foliage and a long flowering season. Just as good are *R.* 'La France', 12 ft (4 m) high, and *R.* 'Madame Grégoire Staechelin', 20 ft (6 m) high.

Ramblers usually have one big burst of small flowers held in large clusters that appear mainly in early summer. They are at their best growing into trees, where their sprays of flowers can cascade over the branches. Alternatively, use any sturdy tall prop like an arch or a bower, preferably an ornamental one that will still be an attractive feature in winter.

The one-burst ramblers include some vigorous growers. *Rosa* 'Paul's Himalayan Musk', 30 ft (10 m) high, will even put on a decent show in the poor, dry soil under a *Leylandii* and will snake through the host plant, turning it into a sensational wall of delicate pink for a couple of weeks in mid-summer. Another impressive rambler is *R. helenae*, which can hook itself over a 20 ft (6 m) hedge, holding up clusters of scented white flowers.

For a very strong, fruity scent, try the robust white *Rosa* 'Bobbie James', 30 ft (10 m), which looks particularly spectacular shooting into and clambering all over an old apple tree. It has heavier flowers than the otherwise similar *R.* 'Rambling Rector'. Other first-rate ramblers include *R.* 'Albéric Barbier', 20 ft (6 m) high, with creamy white flowers; *R.* 'Albertine', 15 ft (5 m) high, with glorious copper-pink blooms; the creamy pink *R.* 'Félicité Perpétuée', 15 ft (5 m) high; *R.* 'Francis E. Lester', 15 ft (5 m) high, with whitish pink flowers; *R.* 'Goldfinch', 10 ft (3 m) high, in yellow; *R.* 'Paul Transon', 15 ft (5 m) high, in copper-orange; and *R.* 'Seagull', 20 ft (6 m) high, in white.

Above left: **Rosa 'Rambling Rector' is a vigorous and robust climbing rose that can reach as high as 25 ft (7.5 m). It is ideal for concealing an ugly building or growing through a tree.**

Above right: **The more modest-sized R. 'Paul's Lemon Pillar' rarely exceeds 15 ft (4.5 m), and is therefore a perfect choice for small gardens. It will flower best when trained against a warm, sunny wall.**

Sweet peas

Sweet peas (*Lathyrus odoratus*) flower from summer to early fall and are available in a wealth of rich colors, from scarlet to white. They have a pure, sweet fragrance that, on a warm, still day, is detectable even from 20–30 ft (6–9 m) away. Flowers of the recently developed Spencer strain are not as strongly scented as those of the older cultivars. The most fragrant are the purple *Lathyrus odoratus*, 6 ft (1.8 m) high, and the 'Old-fashioned' sweet peas of the same height, in blues, reds, pinks, and white, and particularly the wonderful maroon *L. o.* 'Matucana'. Grow sweet peas as annuals from seed, training them up cane wigwams (*see page 74*), or onto horizontal stakes, 5–6 ft (1.5–1.8 m) above ground, supported along their length by vertical sticks. Alternatively, grow them up an arch or spreading over topiary. Dead-head sweet peas regularly for extra flowers.

Other scented climbers

The spring novelty is *Schisandra rubriflora*, 20 ft (6 m) high, from India, Burma, and China. It is surprisingly rarely grown, even though it is an excellent, vigorous climber, and hardy to 14°F (–10°C). The scarlet, downward-facing, lightly scented cupped flowers are followed in the fall—providing both male and female plants are present—by small red fruits resembling a string of beads. The deciduous green leaves, 5 in (12 cm) long, turn yellow before they fall. In a slightly milder, more sheltered garden, where temperatures do not fall below 20°F (–7°C), try *Schisandra sphenanthera*, which has subtle green and beige flowers. Both *Schisandra* species flower in late spring. Since they originate in forests and woodlands, these plants require a partially shady site in humus-rich soil in order to thrive. Grow them up horizontal wires fixed to a wall or posts.

Another equally attractive spring-flowering climber is *Akebia quinata*, known as the chocolate vine. It is semi-evergreen, retaining some leaves over winter, and produces lovely small, cupped, chocolate-maroon flowers. It can reach 30 ft (10 m) and needs training up wires to keep it neat. A single plant produces both male and female flowers with a spicy vanilla scent, but you must hand-pollinate it in spring using a small paintbrush. This climber may also produce sausage-shaped fruits, provided the summer is hot: try growing it against a warm, sunny wall.

If your garden would benefit from a dense evergreen climber with a powerful scent, try *Trachelospermum jasminoides*, which can reach up to 28 ft (9 m) high and produces shiny, dark green foliage and starry, highly scented, white flowers from mid- to late summer. It needs a mild, sheltered garden, where winter temperatures do not drop below 23°F (–5°C), and fertile, well-drained soil. *T. jasminoides* 'Wilsonii' has bronze foliage that turns a rich red shade over winter. *T. asiaticum* is also frost hardy and about 6 ft (1.8 m) shorter, with smaller, gorgeous yellow flowers.

Jasmines have an exquisite, heady scent that lingers in the air in summer. Choose them carefully, since some are frost tender. The deciduous *Jasminum officinale* is fully hardy and is ideal

Opposite page, far left: **Akebia quinata is an attractive, unusual climber. Train it up a wall or let it clamber over a derelict stump. It has small, eye-catching flowers and reaches 30 ft (9 m) high.**

Opposite page, above left: **The sweet pea, Lathyrus odoratus, is the ultimate scented annual. Train it up wigwams of canes.**

for sheltered, warm, sunny walls. It produces white, highly scented flowers and can easily reach an upstairs window, growing at least 25 ft (8 m) high. *J. polyanthum* also has white perfumed flowers, but is half-hardy, so in cool climates needs to be grown in a solarium (*see page 72*).

With its showy, gently honey-scented flowers, the cup-and-saucer vine (*Cobaea scandens*) is an excellent annual climber. It can grow 12 ft (4 m) in a season, so is ideal for quickly filling gaps. Sow the seeds in mid-spring indoors in pots, and gradually acclimatize the seedlings to life outdoors, before planting them against a warm wall. Nip out the top growth to encourage plenty of new shoots, and in summer and fall you will enjoy masses of creamy green fragrant flowers that later turn purple.

Above right: **Trachelospermum jasminoides has three great virtues—it is evergreen, has glossy leaves, and is sweetly scented throughout the second half of the summer. It requires a warm, sheltered garden to flourish.**

Left: **Cobaea scandens is a quick-sprint annual. If there is no supporting wall, let it twine around a shrub.**

SCENTED GALLERY

Akebia quinata
(Chocolate vine)

Height: 30 ft (10 m); leaves: year-round in mild
climates; flowers: early or mid-spring; fully hardy
but can be susceptible to late frosts
Semi-evergreen, twining climber producing
chocolate-purple/maroon flowers with a
gentle vanilla scent and sausage-shaped
fruits. Requires fertile, well-drained soil in
a sunny site. Grow up walls or bowers.
Pruning: Little required, but in spring remove
weak growth, or prune by one-third to
restrict the plant's size.

Clematis armandii

Height: 20ft (6m); leaves: year-round; flowers:
spring; frost hardy
Evergreen twining climber with vanilla-
scented white flowers and copper foliage.
Needs a sheltered, sunny site with well-
drained soil. Use to clothe a fence or wall-
mounted trellis, or to cover an arch, arbor,
or bower. Alternatively clematis can be
grown over a shrub or tree.
Pruning: Group 1 (*see page 76*).

Clematis rehderiana

Height: 22 ft (7 m); flowers: mid-summer to late
autumn; fully hardy
Deciduous twining climber bearing pale or
straw-yellow, downward-facing flowers with
a cowslip-like scent. Needs fertile, well-
drained soil to thrive.
Pruning: Group 3 (*see page 76*).

Clematis × *triternata*
'Rubromarginata'

Height: 12 ft (4 m); flowers: late summer and early
autumn; fully hardy
Deciduous twining climber with fragrant
white, red-edged flowers. Needs fertile,
well-drained soil to thrive.
Pruning: Group 3 (*see page 76*).

Jasminum officinale
(Common jasmine)

Height: 25 ft (8 m), or more in favorable
conditions; flowers: summer; frost hardy
Deciduous twining climber producing
abundant white, strongly scented flowers.
Needs fertile, well-drained soil. Give a

high-potash tomato feed in summer, which
encourages the plant to flower prolifically.
Grows up any garden structure.
Pruning: After flowering, cut back flowered
shoots to a strong stem.

Lathyrus odoratus and cultivars
(Sweet peas)

Height: 6 ft (1.8 m); flowers: summer to early
autumn; fully hardy
Annuals climbing mainly by their leaf
tendrils, available in a wide color range and
rich scents, especially the 'Old-fashioned'
types. Sow presoaked seeds in early spring
in pots, using potting medium. When 3 in
(7 cm) high, or when they have two pairs of
leaves, pinch out the tops of seedlings;
harden off outside, and plant out. Best in
humus-rich, fertile soil, and thrives and
flowers best in full sun.

Lonicera japonica 'Halliana'
(Honeysuckle)

Height: 30 ft (10 m); leaves: year-round; flowers:
summer to autumn; fully hardy

Evergreen twining climber bearing white,
richly scented flowers. Requires humus-rich,
free-draining soil in sun or dappled shade.
Also needs plenty of water in summer and a
thick spring mulch. Grow up walls and trees.
Pruning: Prune mature plants by one-third
each spring, or every other spring.

Rosa 'Gloire de Dijon'

Height: 15 ft (5 m); flowers: summer; fully hardy
Deciduous, vigorous climbing rose with buff-
yellow flowers. Like all roses, best on fertile,
humus-rich, well-drained but moist soil.
If possible, plant against a shady wall.
Otherwise, train against a wall or fence, or
over an arch, arbor, or bower. Can be leggy,
so grow shrubs at its base.
Pruning: *see page 76*.

Rosa 'Guinée'

Height: 15 ft (5 m); flowers: summer; fully hardy
Deciduous climbing rose producing very
dark purple-red flowers. Train against a wall
or fence, or over a garden structure.
Pruning: *see page 76*.

Above left: **Lonicera japonica 'Halliana'**

Above right: **Clematis armandii**

Left: **Akebia quinata**

Below left: **Jasminum officinale**

Right: **Lathyrus 'Spencer Waved Mixed'**

Opposite page: **Rosa 'Gloire de Dijon'**

Rosa 'Paul Transon'

Height: 15 ft (5 m); flowers: summer; fully hardy

Rambling rose with copper-orange buds and slightly pinker flowers, set off by bright, shiny foliage. Like all roses, best on fertile, humus-rich, well-drained but moist soil.
Pruning: *see page 76.*

Schisandra rubrifolia

Height: 20 ft (6 m); flowers: spring; fully hardy

Deciduous twining climber producing scarlet flowers that are followed by red, beadlike fruits. Thrives in fertile, moist but well-drained soil in sun or light shade. Grow into trees or over a fence or trellis.
Pruning: Thin as required in spring.

Wisteria floribunda 'Macrobotrys'

Height: 28 ft (9 m) or more in favorable conditions; flowers: early summer; fully hardy

Deciduous twining climber with showy, blue-violet flowers in racemes 3 ft (90 cm) long or more. Requires fertile, well-drained soil, ideally in sun but will tolerate some shade.
Pruning: *see page 77.*

Wisteria sinensis 'Alba'

Height: 28 ft (9 m), or more in favorable conditions; flowers: late spring; fully hardy

Deciduous twining climber with sensational white flowers. Needs fertile, well-drained soil, preferably in a sunny site but tolerates some shade. Spectacular grown over arches, making long tunnels draped with flowers.
Pruning: *see page 77.*

Far left: **Schisandra rubrifolia**
Left: **Wisteria floribunda 'Macrobotrys'**

One of the greatest assets of climbers is their ability to act as a screen: they provide privacy and can conceal unattractive structures in the garden. Evergreens are particularly useful for giving cover in winter, while some deciduous climbers have colorful autumn foliage.

FOLIAGE

Evergreen climbers and shrubs

The Chilean *Hydrangea serratifolia*, 15 ft (5 m) or more, is one of the best self-clinging evergreens, climbing by aerial roots that lock on to adjacent walls, tree trunks, or any other potential support. Surprisingly—and undeservedly—underrated, it grows up shady walls happily, forming a dense network of branches and leathery leaves, 6 in (15 cm) long, and producing white flowers in late summer. Evergreen hydrangeas are frost hardy and require a warm, sheltered garden, unlike the deciduous hydrangeas, which tolerate colder weather. Equally underrated is the attractive *Pileostegia viburnoides*, 20 ft (6 m) high. It has beautiful leathery foliage with a big burst of creamy white flowers from the end of summer to early autumn. It also climbs by aerial roots, and thrives in fertile, free-draining soil in sun or light shade. Both *H. serratifolia* and *P. viburnoides* require strong, stout structures to support their weight.

Some *Rubus* species are terrific climbers, hauling themselves over shrubs and walls, and anchoring themselves in place with their prickles. The 10 ft (3 m) high *Rubus flagelliflorus*, with white flowers and edible black berries, has long graceful stems

Above left: **The Chilean climber, *Mutisia ilicifolia*, is slightly tender. However, in cold regions, it can be grown as an annual or cut back in autumn and potted up indoors to over-winter.**

Right: **The shiny, evergreen, Chinese *Holboellia coriacea*. is a worthwhile plant to grow in a garden with a warm, sheltered wall. Be warned— it will not survive icy spells if it is exposed to the full blast of winter weather.**

Evergreen clematis like *Clematis armandii* provide interest in the winter border.

bearing large, dark green leaves: tie it to an arbor or tree stump. If you have a large garden, opt for *R. henryi*, which grows twice as high and has deep glossy foliage. Both are evergreen and thrive in full sun. Annually, in spring, prune half the stems close to the base—about 12 in (30 cm) above the ground—to force new flowering shoots the following year.

Several clematis are evergreen and will provide interest in the border over winter; but if you intend to create a screen, bear in mind that clematis will not provide a thick, all-obscuring growth. *Clematis armandii* (see pages 12, 22 and Group 1, page 76) is a good evergreen climber, as is *C. cirrhosa* var. *balearica* (Group 3, see page 76). Its striking dark green leaves, with glossy undersides, turn bronze in winter, and are accompanied by relatively insignificant yellowish flowers. Grow *C. c.* var. *balearica* in a sheltered, warm site, and provide a support for its 15 ft (5 m) high stems. The new *C. c.* var. *balearica* 'Freckles' has larger white flowers with red markings.

For gardens where temperatures do not fall below 23°F (−5°C), try *Holboellia coriacea* or *Mutisia ilicifolia*. *H. coriacea* is a Chinese twiner that grows naturally in shady woodland. It easily reaches 20 ft (6 m), and produces attractive foliage and strongly scented but insignificant spring flowers. Plant it near a strong, sturdy structure such as a wall, and prune in spring to

Above left: **The shrubby, climbing *Euonymus fortunei* 'Silver Queen' is a handsome shrub. It requires occasional smartening up with judicious pruning; otherwise, it can become rather unshapely.**

Above right: **The evergreen *Clematis cirrhosa* is an early-flowering clematis. The milder and more sheltered the garden, the more likely this clematis is to flourish. It has yellowish, bell-shaped winter flowers followed by feathery seed heads.**

maintain its shape. *Mutisia ilicifolia*, from South America, is a smaller tendril-climbing evergreen, 10 ft (3 m) high. It produces wonderful pink, daisylike flowers in summer, and small spiny leaves. Plant it in well-drained soil in a sunny site, with its roots in the shade. Growing it through a shrub is ideal, although walls and strong trellises are also fine. In spring, prune lightly since these plants dislike being severely cut back. The frost-hardy *M. decurrens* is also an evergreen climber of great merit, but is less commonly available.

In addition to the true climbers, there are several shrubs that act as climbers, growing happily up any vertical surfaces. *Euonymus fortunei* and its cultivars are semiprostrate shrubs for the border, but they will climb up to reach 3–5 m (10–15 ft) if given support such as a wall. They all thrive in semishady beds, and their shiny green leaves are ideal for brightening up gloomy areas of the garden. The variegated forms include *E. f.* 'Emerald 'n' Gold', which is green and yellow, tinged pink in winter; *E. f.* 'Silver Queen', which is bright yellow in spring, later becoming green and white, turning slightly pink in winter; and *E. f.* 'Harlequin', some of whose leaves can be albino. The leaves of *E. f.* 'Coloratus' turn purple-red in winter. Prune *E. fortunei* and its cultivars after flowering to keep growth in check and maintain the plant's shape.

Ivies

Often overlooked, ivies make excellent garden plants. There are over three hundred types available: all are evergreen, and they are incredibly versatile and diverse. While some are star performers and worth growing in their own right, most are ideal as the "chorus," their foliage providing a luxuriant backdrop to other plantings. They are grown mainly for their leaves, but when they reach the maximum height for their support, they should flower and produce fruit.

There is no need to tie ivies in: just nudge them in the right direction, and they will cling as they go. They need a sturdy support unless regularly trimmed, since they can become tangled and heavy. They are fine growing up mature trees, but keep them away from young trees, as well as gutters and window frames. Also bear in mind that they can damage a crumbly wall. Prune as hard as you like in spring, preferably on new growth, to maintain the plant's shape. You can grow ivies in various sites, and on soils ranging from poor to humus-rich, preferably with good drainage.

Ivies vary greatly in vigor: some grow rapidly, others very slowly. They are also available in a wide variety of leaf shapes, both large and small: some are diamond-, fan- or heart-shaped, others resemble bird's feet or are curly at the edges. The leaf

Opposite page: Often underrated, ivies have become last-resort climbers whereas some, such as this *Hedera helix* 'Goldheart', are multitalented. It has the most striking yellow marking of any ivy, keeps its stylish looks throughout winter, is the only yellow variegated ivy suitable for shade, and reaches 25 ft (8 m) high.

This page: Ivies can be grown up sturdy trees, such as this silver birch, or over a house wall. Do not let them reach the crown of a tree in their weighty adult phase as a top-heavy tree can get blown down. The leaves of ivies are not poisonous, but the seeds should be avoided.

shape also depends on the age of the plant: when young, most species usually produce leaves that are lobed, but when they become adult, they tend to produce unlobed leaves.

The color range and patterning on the leaves of ivies are also highly variable. *Hedera helix* 'Angularis Aurea' is yellow in spring, and chocolate brown in winter; *H. h.* 'Glacier' produces purple-red stems; the leaves of *H. h.* 'Goldheart' have large yellow markings; and those of *H. h.* 'Helvetica' turn red in winter. The all-green-leafed ivies tolerate shade, while the variegated kinds prefer more light.

Hedera helix is a particularly useful ivy, since it will thrive in amazingly poor conditions. Even in a cool, gloomy, damp corner of the garden, it will rapidly grow as high as 25 ft (8 m), producing masses of shiny green foliage. It is also wonderfully quirky and variable, offering a great diversity of leaf form. *H. h.* subsp. *hibernica* is more like a climbing hedge, making growth about 12 in (35 cm) deep; if you want to keep your garage warm in winter, this is the climber to choose.

Ivy can clothe an unattractive surface quickly and provides an excellent foil for other plants: reds, yellows, and whites stand out particularly well against the green. To cover a large area— such as a wall or fence—choose *Hedera colchica*, which has 10 in (25 cm) long leaves, and a growth span of 30 ft (10 m).

Most ivies are ideal as the "chorus," their foliage providing a luxuriant backdrop to other plantings.

H. c. 'Dentata Variegata' is useful for walls that lack sun and generally reaches 15 ft (5 m) high. It has gray-green leaves, 6 in (15 cm) long, with bright creamy yellow margins, and smells of gin when crushed. *H.* subsp. *hibernica* has slightly smaller leaves and grows twice as high, also making it useful for wall cover.

Ivy also doubles as a first-rate hedge filler. *Hedera helix* 'Atropurpurea' livens up a drab hedge with its dark purple winter foliage, as does *H. canariensis* 'Gloire de Marengo', which has gorgeous dark green leaves with silvery flecks and white edging. The latter needs a warm wall in a mild area if it is to be evergreen; in a borderline winter it loses its leaves, although it recovers quickly as soon as spring arrives.

There are numerous other imaginative ways of growing ivy, some of which add a formal or elegant note to the garden. Send them up 10 ft (3 m) high poles and stand them at the back of a bed, or place them 6 ft (1.8 m) apart, encircling a pond; alternatively, use them to filter a view. You could also grow ivies over a row of tall, wide arching hoops covered in a strong, tight net, making a tunnel into another part of the yard, or even make an ivy castle using a strong metal frame. Ivies are also useful for growing around statuary, particularly new pieces, since they soften the outline and detract from the brightness of the stone or concrete to provide a sense of timelessness.

Ivies are excellent for training as topiary shapes. Create a three-dimensional wire frame shaped like a rabbit or penguin, anything with a flowing, rounded outline, then pack it with moist

Use ivy in imaginative ways to add a formal or elegant note to the garden, training it up vertical poles sited at the back of a bed or over a row of tall, arching hoops to form a tunnel into another part of the yard.

sphagnum moss and soilless potting medium. Plant ivy cuttings 6 in (15 cm) apart, and pinch out the side shoots to make them develop plenty of branchlets. *Hedera helix* 'Ivalace' or *H. h.* 'Miniature Needlepoint' are both ideal for topiary: the smaller the leaf, the more well-defined the design will be. Avoid large-leafed species such as *H. colchica* 'Dentata'.

Opposite page, left: **A dovecote is a good garden focal point. Make use of it as a vertical support to train a climbing plant, such as ivy, whose stems will cascade over the edges.**

Opposite page, right: **For detailed topiary shapes, use a medium-, or small-leafed ivy, such as the fast-growing *Hedera helix* 'Ivalace', which has crimped margins.**

Above: *Hedera canariensis* **'Gloire de Marengo' is a fast-growing variegated ivy. Its foliage provides a stunning contrast with an autumn-reddening Virginia creeper.**

Climbers often give their most stunning foliage effects in the fall, covering walls, fences, and trellises in rich shades of purple, crimson, burnt orange, and gold.

Climbers for autumn color

Many climbers put on their best show in the fall, with their leaves turning magnificent shades of red, orange, yellow, and purple. The degree of brilliance varies from plant to plant, and is determined by a combination of several different factors including autumn light levels, night temperatures, soil fertility, and the length of the preceding winter.

Among the best climbers for autumn color are the parthenocissus vines, which produce sticky pads at the tips of the tendrils and latch onto fences, trees, or any other available support. Boston Ivy (*Parthenocissus tricuspidata*) is highly vigorous and can cover a 50 ft (15 m) wall with three-fingered leaves that roar as red as a furnace for three weeks. Virginia creeper (*P. quinquefolia*), with its finely divided five-fingered foliage is slightly less rampant. Chinese Virginia creeper (*P. henryana*) is a lesser-known, smaller vine, reaching only 20 ft (6 m). Grown for its handsome foliage, it has three- to five- fingered, pointed leaves in soft velvet green, veined white, and turn a fiery shade of red in the fall. All *Parthenocissus* species and cultivars are splendid adorning house walls, but cut them back to avoid damage to your roofs and gutters. Alternatively, send a parthenocissus up into a large mature tree: its stems will dangle down like long red ribbons in the fall. Cut all parthenocissus vines back in early winter when they get out of hand and, if necessary, also in summer.

The *Vitis* genus of grapevines are frequently grown for their ornamental foliage, often with magnificent fall colors; some also produce edible grapes. The white *Vitis vinifera* 'Madeleine Angevine' and the black *V.* 'Brant' turn rich plum and bronze-red shades in autumn and are fully hardy. Most species are fully hardy, but some, such as *V.* 'Pirovano 14', require the warmth of a greenhouse in cooler climates. Other first-rate vines for autumn color include: *V. amurensis*, reaching 40 ft (12 m), with 12 in (30 cm) long leaves; *V. coignetiae*, which can clamber 50 ft (15 m), easily reaching the crown of a tree; the shorter *V. vinifera*, at just 22 ft (7 m) high, and its cultivar that excels in autumn, *V. vinifera* 'Purpurea' with blood-purple foliage. All vines can be reined in if they become too much of a good thing by pruning in mid-winter and again in midsummer if necessary.

Top left: **It is chlorophyll that gives leaves their dominant green color so when chlorophyll levels fall at the end of summer, previously obscured pigments— including red, orange, yellow, and purple—are revealed. The roaring autumnal red of this *Parthenocissus tricuspidata* is actually the result of dying leaf tissue. This climbing plant can reach 50 ft (15 m), and makes an amazing display.**

Above: **The five-fingered leaves of *Parthenocissus quinquefolia* provide a luxuriant autumn show.**

Left: **This mixed planting features bamboo foliage, *Parthenocissus quinquefolia*, ivy, and the evergreen *Clematis armandii*.**

Climbers with fruit

Several climbers are grown for their ornamental fruits, some of which are edible, such as the deciduous *Actinidia deliciosa*, which produces kiwi fruit. The fruit is produced in the fall, and ripens every three years. It is sweet-tasting, provided the summers are hot or the plants are grown under glass; they tolerate cold winters, but can be damaged by frost in late winter. To produce fruit, both a male and female plant are needed, or a self-fertile cultivar. In the right conditions, *A. deliciosa* can shoot past 30 ft (10 m);

however, the plants may be pruned to 12 ft (4 m), and can be grown in a large conservatory. Note the strict pruning regime (*see page 75*). *A. kolomikta* rarely fruits, but has stunning foliage: the young leaves are bronze, turning pink and white in the sun. Protect the new growth from cats who will revel in chewing the young stems, and it should reach 10 ft (3 m) high.

Above: **The golden foliage of *Humulus lupulus* 'Aureus' combines well with *Rosa gallica* 'Complicata', which has single pink blooms and large leaves. It becomes a mini climber, 10 ft (3 m) high.**

Right: **The female flowers, or hops, of the common hop, *Humulus lupulus* 'Aureus', have tiny glands containing chemicals called humulones that are used to give beer its bitter flavor.**

The deciduous common hop (*Humulus lupulus* 'Aureus') is grown mainly for its brightly colored foliage and flowers, which are useful in flower arranging; it fruits in the fall. It is a quick sprinter, climbing 10 ft (3 m) in spring, twice that by the end of the season, and is perfect for filling a corner or covering fences and tree stumps. The foliage is golden-yellow and vinelike, and the female flowers, produced in summer, are used for brewing beer.

The final fall fruiter is *Ampelopsis brevipedunculata*. Its leaves are similar to those of the common hop, and it also grows to 15 ft (5 m), but has masses of blue berries that are particularly noticeable after the leaves have fallen. It needs a sheltered site, preferably against a sunny wall, and wires or a trellis for support. When the sun strikes the berries, their glorious color looks particularly spectacular.

Below left: *Ampelopsis brevipedunculata* outscores the common hop with its blue berries in autumn. Do not be tempted by the shorter *A. b.* 'Elegans' unless you plan to grow it indoors—it will not survive the cold.

Below right: *Actinidia kolomikta* needs a long, hot summer to produce fruit. The young bronze foliage turns pink and white in the sun.

Fruit—edible or purely ornamental—is an additional benefit provided by some climbers, bringing color to the garden after most plants have finished flowering.

FOLIAGE GALLERY

Actinidia deliciosa (Kiwi fruit)

Height: 30 ft (10 m); flowers: summer; fruit: autumn; frost hardy to fully hardy

Deciduous twining climber grown for its striking, often variegated foliage, flowers, and kiwi fruit. Grow up a strong supporting structure like a sheltered, sunny wall, in fertile, free-draining soil. Give tomato fertilizer during the growing season.
Pruning: Prune in late winter to restrict growth by cutting back side shoots to within three or four buds of the main stem.

Ampelopsis brevipedunculata

Height: 15 ft (5 m); flowers: summer; berries: autumn; fully hardy

Deciduous tendril climber with abundant foliage, and producing small green flowers followed by blue berries. Needs fertile, moist but well-drained soil. For a good display of berries, grow on a warm, sunny wall or a robust structure, such as a tree or arbor.
Pruning: Cut back to restrict size in spring. To cover a large surface, prune as for *Vitis coignetiae* (*see below*).

Euonymus fortunei and cultivars

Height: 15 ft (5 m); leaves: year-round; flowers: midsummer; fruit: autumn to winter; fully hardy

Evergreen scrambling climbers bearing bright foliage with variable leaf colorings. Greenish flowers followed by white fruit. Tolerates poor soil. Grow up walls or trees.
Pruning: Cut back in spring for shape.

Hedera colchica 'Dentata Variegata' (Persian ivy)

Height: 15 ft (5 m); leaves: year-round; flowers: autumn (adult stage only); fruit: winter (adult stage only); fully hardy

Evergreen, clinging by aerial roots, with large, variegated leaves. Tolerant but prefers fertile, well-drained soil. Ideal for shady walls.
Pruning: Cut back to size in spring. Avoid cutting into four-year-old, or older, wood.

Hedera helix 'Atropurpurea' (Purple-leafed ivy)

Height: 25 ft (8 m); leaves: year-round; flowers: autumn (adult stage only); fruit: winter (adult stage only); fully hardy

Evergreen, self-clinging climber with dark green foliage turning purple in cold weather.
Pruning: *see Hedera colchica* 'Dentata Variegata' (*above*).

Humulus lupulus 'Aureus'

Height: 20 ft (6 m); flowers: mid- to late summer; fruit: autumn; fully hardy

Twining perennial with bright yellow foliage and hops (female flowers). Best in sun or dappled shade in humus-rich, well-drained soil. Grow up a strong tripod or over a wall.
Pruning: Cut to the ground in late fall.

Hydrangea serratifolia

Height: 15 ft (5 m); leaves: year-round; flowers: late summer; frost hardy

Evergreen climber clinging by aerial roots. Produces a good show of leathery leaves and white flowers. Needs a sheltered spot in sun or dappled shade, and a moderately fertile, moist, but well-drained humus-rich soil. Grow up strong, stout supporting structures such as walls.
Pruning: Cut back in spring.

Parthenocissus quinquefolia (Virginia creeper)

Height: up to 50 ft (15 m); leaves: fiery red in fall; fully hardy

Deciduous tendril climber with orange-red leaves in fall. Likes sun and shade, and fertile, well-drained soil. Nearly indestructible. Good for large surfaces like walls and trees.
Pruning: Nip back new plants to encourage fresh shoots. Thereafter, prune in early winter and, if necessary, in summer to check growth.

Vitis coignetiae (Grapevine)

Height: up to 50 ft (15 m); leaves: autumn color; fruit: autumn; fully hardy

Deciduous tendril climber with bright red foliage and unpalatable black fruits. Thrives in sun or dappled shade, and needs humus-rich, well-drained soil. Grow up strong structures like walls, arbors and trees.
Pruning: In the first winter, cut back stems by one-third to one-half, and remove the weakest shoots. Thereafter, prune new growth in winter by one-half. When plant fills its allotted space, prune to restrict size.

Top left:
Humulus lupulus 'Aureus'

Top center:
Actinidia deliciosa

Top right:
Vitis cognetiae

Above:
Parthenocissus quinquefolia

Far left:
Hedera colchica 'Dentata Variegata'

Left:
Ampelopsis brevipedunculata

Opposite page:
Actinidia kolomikta

Every garden, however small, should include some climbing plants. They perform the vital task of clothing featureless walls or other vertical structures, and provide swathes of color when in bloom. Flowering climbers can interweave with other plants to extend the season of interest.

FLOWERS

Early-flowering clematis

Throughout spring, clematis reign supreme among all the climbers. There are different types of clematis to flower right through the season, providing a colorful backdrop to the emerging spring bulbs. Clematis are often planted singly, with plenty of space around each plant; however, if closely planted, two clematis of similar vigor and contrasting flower colors can look extremely effective whipping around each other. All of the following clematis are deciduous, preferring a warm, sunny, sheltered site, and are in Group 1 (*see page 76*) for pruning. (*See also Scented climbers, pages 12–13.*) The flower forms of different clematis species are very varied, and include nodding bells, open bells, and single, semidouble, and double flowers.

Clematis alpina and its cultivars are excellent climbers and are among the first clematis to come into bloom, flowering from mid- to late spring. They do not exceed 10–12 ft (3–4 m), and look very beautiful when encouraged to scramble over a small tree, shrub, balustrade or low wall. All of the following have nodding, lanternlike flowers: *C. alpina* and *C. a.* 'Frances Rivis' (with the largest flowers), in a rich mid-blue; *C. a.* 'Columbine',

in a cool light blue; *C. a.* 'Helsingborg', in a bold, clear, deep violet; the long-flowering *C. a.* 'Pink Flamingo', in pale pink; and *C. a.* subsp. *sibirica* 'White Moth', in pristine white.

Flowering slightly later, and prolonging the clematis show of springtime color, are *Clematis macropetala* and its cultivars. They also have nodding, bell-like flowers, grow up to 12 ft (4 m) high, and are particularly useful since they are able to withstand shade. The species *C. macropetala* has violet-blue, quite showy flowers, but if you yearn for bold, beautiful colors, its cultivars are even more striking, especially the sugar-pink, free-flowering *C.m.* 'Markham's Pink', 10 ft (3 m) high, and the rich mid-blue *C. m.* 'Maidwell Hall', reaching 6½ ft (2 m) high. *C. m.* 'Lagoon' is a vibrant, deep dark blue, and slightly taller. All are first-rate climbers, with extremely decorative, fluffy silver seedheads following the flowers.

Opposite page, top right: ***Clematis macropetala* was first introduced to Britain in 1910 from northern China and Siberia. It is hardy, with violet-blue flowers and seedheads throughout late summer and autumn.**

Opposite page, below left: **The pale, lavender-blue flowers of 'Maidwell Hall', a cultivar of *Clematis macropetala*, have exotic-looking flowers.**

Left: ***Clematis* 'The President' has rich purple flowers, touched with blue. It blooms in three bursts from late spring to early autumn, and reaches 10 ft (3 m) high.**

Right: **The flowers of *Clematis macropetala* are offset by the foliage of the ivy, *Hedera helix* 'Buttercup'.**

Below: ***Clematis* 'Niobe' has starry, scarlet flowers through summer and early fall.**

Clematis for mid-spring and early-summer color

By mid-spring the vigorous species *Clematis montana* and its cultivars begin to bloom. Besides those mentioned on pages 12–13, try *C. m. grandiflora*, with large, 4 in (10 cm) wide white flowers, or *C. m.* 'Tetrarose' in purple-pink. They flower for about four weeks, but are highly prolific and put on a wonderful performance during this time, although some plants might take a few years to get going and flower well.

Clematis chrysocoma has a big burst of faint pink flowers in late spring and flowers sporadically until the fall. The buds, stems, and leaflets have a downy covering. In the wild, it can reach 50 ft (15 m), but in yards, it is more likely to reach 15 ft (5 m)

or so. It needs excellent drainage and a protective mulch around the stem to protect against severe winter chills. Similar but hardier is the pink *C. × vedrariensis*.

Flowering from late spring to late-summer, often with subsequent bursts, are the large-flowered clematis cultivars with single, fully double, or semidouble flowers. There are just under one hundred cultivars to choose from. All are deciduous and fully hardy to frost hardy. All are in Group 2 (*see page 76*). Most reach about 10 ft (3 m) high, and the first flush of flowers are often 10 in (25 cm) wide. Colors include white (*C*. 'Henryi' and the more vigorous *C*. 'Marie Boisselot'); pale pink (*C*. 'Nelly Moser' and the more strongly colored sugar-pink *C*. 'Bee's Jubilee'); blue verging on lilac (*C*. 'Mrs. Cholmondeley', *C*. 'Général Sikorski', *C*. 'Lasurstern', and the vigorous *C*. 'Vyvyan Pennell'); rich violet-blue to purple (*C*. 'Daniel Deronda', *C*. 'Horn of Plenty', and *C*. 'The President'); and bold, vivid red (*C*. 'Niobe').

Late-flowering clematis include vibrant shades of rich pink, red, and purple.

Summer-flowering clematis

In summer and early fall, some of the most beautiful of all the clematis come into flower. They tend to flower higher up the stem than other clematis, about 4–5 ft (1.2–1. 5 m) above ground, so consider this when planning their role in your garden. They are mostly deciduous and all fall into Group 3 (*see page 76*).

Within the group are numerous large-flowered cultivars, many of them real stunners, all fully hardy and with single flowers. Perhaps the most enduringly popular of all the summer-flowering clematis is the colorful and prolific *Clematis* 'Jackmanii Superba' (also known as *C.* 'Jackmanii'), in a rich, velvety, imperial purple hue; *C.* 'Gipsy Queen' is also deep purple in color. The bright mauve-pink *C.* 'Comtesse de Bouchaud', 10 ft (3 m) high, is spectacular, as is *C.* 'Ernest Markham', 12 ft (4 m) high, one of the best reds of all the clematis. Another superb red is the slightly smaller *C.* 'Ville de Lyon', which reaches 10 ft (3 m)—ideal for smaller gardens. *C.* 'Victoria' starts off rosy-mauve, then becomes darker, and reaches 10 ft (3 m) high. The blue *C.* 'Perle d'Azur', raised in France over 100 years ago, is taller, at 12 ft (4 m) high.

Clematis viticella and its cultivars produce exquisite, small, bell-shaped flowers from late-summer into autumn. The plants need to be cut down to 9 in (23 cm) above ground in spring, so are ideal positioned to flower above spring- to early summer-performing shrubs. They are all fully hardy and resistant to clematis wilt. The species *C. viticella* has elegant, nodding purple flowers, 1½ in (3.5 cm) across, on long stalks, while the cultivars have slightly larger flowers, 2–3 in (5–8 cm) across. *C. v.* 'Alba Luxurians' is vigorous with pure white flowers; *C. v.* 'Etoile Violette' is an alluring dark purple; the wonderful *C. v.* 'Kermesina' has deep wine-red flowers; *C. v.* 'Madame Julia Correvon' is another rich, deep red; and *C. v.* 'Royal Velours' is wine-purple. All are 10 ft (3 m) high except *C. v.* 'Etoile Violette', at 12 ft (4 m) high. *C. texensis* 'Etoile Rose' is also a first-rate clematis, producing superb nodding, bell-shaped flowers in rich pink from mid- through to late summer.

Opposite page:

Top left: **The large-flowering** *Clematis* **'Jackmanii Superba' is an 1878 sport of** *Clematis* **'Jackmanii'. The vivid purple blooms darken slightly before fading.**

Top right: **The white-flowered** *Clematis viticella* **'Alba Luxurians' is a cultivar of the species C.** *viticella* **that was introduced into England in the 16th century.**

Center left: *Clematis* **'Comtesse de Bouchaud' is a prolific, large-flowered mauve-pink hybrid that blooms through early- and midsummer. It was introduced in 1900.**

Center right: *Clematis* **'Kermesina' has flowers of a gorgeous rich red. For a stylish contrast, grow it through the catkinlike racemes of the evergreen shrub,** *Itea ilicifolia.*

Below: **The flowers of** *Clematis* **'Etoile Violette' have a contrasting creamy eye.**

This page: *Clematis* **'Ville de Lyon' has delightful deep-red flowers. Grow it through a shrub; the lower foliage can fall by midsummer, and the stems are best hidden.**

Opposite page: *Rosa* 'Bantry Bay' is perfect for growing up pillars because it is not a prolific sprinter but instead makes a restrained clump.

Left: With startling orange-red blooms to brighten a north wall, *Rosa* 'Danse du Feu' flowers into the fall.

There are numerous magnificent climbing and rambling roses that offer great intensity of color.

Summer roses

Exquisitely beautiful and highly diverse, roses are invaluable in the garden over summer. Besides the strongly scented varieties (*see pages 18–19*), there are numerous magnificent climbing and rambling roses with single to fully double flowers that offer great intensity of color and variety of form. Several repeat-flower into the fall. For pruning details, turn to page 75.

Rosa 'Parkdirektor Riggers' gives strong red color all summer on 12 ft (4 m) high growth. Planted to grow over an arbor, it creates a vibrant walkway or bower. Other colorful climbers, all about 10 ft (3 m) high, include the pink *R.* 'Bantry Bay'; *R.* 'Danse du Feu', in orange scarlet, with dozens of sprays of medium-size flowers; and buff-yellow *R.* 'Penny Rose'.

Large structures and eyesores need more rampant, swamping growth. The gothic arbor in the center of the white garden at Sissinghurst, Kent, England, is covered by a stupendous *Rosa mulliganii*. It is extremely vigorous, growing 25 ft (8 m) high, and is covered with a mass of small white flowers. The yellow *R.* 'Mermaid' can also cover 25 ft (8 m), but is not as hardy. It needs a warm, sheltered site and is evergreen in mild winters.

For growing through trees, choose vigorous roses such as *Rosa* 'Belvedere', which can reach 40 ft (12 m) high, with large panicles of pink flowers, and the equally delightful shorter pink *R.* 'Mme. Butterfly, Climbing', at 20 ft (6 m). Many buildings are very much enhanced by roses growing up their walls to provide flower color and sweet, welcoming fragrance. For example, *R.* 'Alister Stella Gray' produces yellow flowers that combine well with those of the wonderful *R.* 'Rose-Marie Viaud', which opens bright cerise and fades to gentle lilac. Both are 15 ft (5 m) high.

Above: *Rosa* 'Parkdirektor Riggers' produces vibrant red flowers all summer, has glossy, dark green foliage, and is perfect for growing over an arbor. It is not fragrant, however, and can be prone to an occasional attack of black spot.

Far left: ***Ipomoea purpurea*** **is a stunning purple-flowered annual climber. It is a weed in the tropics and subtropics.** *I. batatas* **is the sweet potato, while the seeds of** *I. tricolor* **were used as a hallucinogen by the Aztecs.**

Left: ***Solanum jasminoides*** **'Album' scrambles up walls, producing longer-lasting flowers than the species. Its delicate white blooms mix well with** *Ipomoea purpurea.*

Summer twisters and twiners

The big summer display comes from roses and clematis, but there are numerous other highly versatile summer climbers. Any of the following may be encouraged to twine around canes and poles, whip through shrubs and tall vertical plants, or cover walls. Bear in mind that they do not need a whole wall to themselves; indeed, several climbers grown together can offer pleasing combinations of color and form.

Solanum is a vast genus, consisting of about 1,400 species, several of which are climbers. Among the best are the pale blue summer- and autumn-flowering South American *Solanum jasminoides*, or its stylish white forms, *S. j.* 'Album' and *S. j.* 'Album Variegatum'. They all grow to approximately 15 ft (5 m) high, prefer a warm, sunny site, and are half hardy, although you can grow them as annuals in colder climates. As a precaution, take summer cuttings, keeping them indoors over winter, and planting them out next spring. Alternatively, give the plant a protective winter mulch. Provided it has survived the winter, *S. j.* 'Album' will flower as early as late spring.

Solanum jasminoides and its cultivars are useful in the garden for combining with other plants to flesh out a planting plan: grow them against a wall with purple clematis, flowing

into the border to twine around the purple perennial *Verbena bonariensis*, 6 ft (2 m) high, or the spires of the purple *Malva sylvestris* subsp. *mauritanica*, or an arching *Buddleia*. They are also excellent for larger, more dramatic displays: plant them to weave around a tall standard fuchsia, surrounded by bright yellow *Lilium* 'Citronella' above the long, stabbing leaves of a cordyline. Alternatively, tie them to an arbor or front-door post.

Try also the frost-hardy violet *Solanum crispum* 'Glasnevin', 20 ft (6 m) high, which has a slightly longer flowering period than *S. jasminoides* and thrives in chalky soil. It is not necessary to tie it to a wall; instead, leave it to form a great twirling mound in the border. The remaining *Solanum* species are frost tender, so keep them under glass over winter in cold climates, or take cuttings. *S. rantonnetii* is purple and grows 5 ft (1.5 m) high; *S. wendlandii* is a pretty lilac blue and the same height; while *S. seaforthianum* has blue, purple, pink or white flowers and grows as much as four times as high. These plants may be placed informally around the garden.

Common morning glory (*Ipomoea purpurea*) is a fabulous, not-too-rampant, 12 ft (4 m) high twining climber with gorgeous, bright purple flowers. It has many excellent cultivars, including the

blue *Ipomoea purpurea* 'Dickensonii' and the magenta *I. p.* 'Kermesiana'. They need a warm, sheltered position and fertile soil. Train them around tall lollipop shapes beside a path; alternatively, grow them in pots to climb above other summer pot plants like the impressive carmine *Geranium maderense*, with 24 in (60 cm) long dissected leaves, begonias, or *Solenostemon* 'Royal Scot' with bold, flashy leaves in dark red with apricot patches and gold margins. The azure *I. tricolor* 'Heavenly Blue' is another excellent, richly colored climber. To grow ipomoea from seed, sow in the spring and pinch out the growing tips of young plants to produce more growth.

For late-season color, try the exquisite star-shaped, pale blue South American *Tweedia caerulea*, which twines 6½ ft (2 m) high. It also makes good cut flowers. *T. caerulea* is frost tender and requires fertile, well-drained soil. Sow seed in spring. The twining tropical African black-eyed Susan (*Thunbergia alata*), also frost tender, grows about 10 ft (3 m) from spring seed. Its yellow or orange flowers with black centers climb over shrubs and up through other climbers. In cool climates it is always best to grow pots of these colorful annuals under glass, then bring them out in early summer, positioning them all around the garden to add vibrant spots of color.

Violet twining snapdragons (*Maurandella antirrhiniflora*) are marvelous climbers that need stakes or a trellis to whip through. They grow 3–6½ ft (90 cm–2 m) high, with rich violet flowers outside, white inside, from summer to autumn. *Maurandya barclayana* grows about 4 ft (1.2 m) taller in white, pink, or purple, and *Lophospermum erubescens*, 10 ft (3 m) high, is rose-pink with trumpet-shaped flowers. All are bright, lively climbers for training through gaps in a hot, sunny site.

Among the greatest of the twisters and twiners are members of the *Tropaeolum* genus, which excel at scrambling through and over hedges, where they run along the surface, disappear from sight, then emerge farther along. They flower in vivid reds, oranges, and yellows, in summer to fall, and some are perennials, with underground storage organs.

Left: **Solanum crispum 'Glasnevin' has shrubby growth, making it an efficient gap-filler in the border. It is the hardiest of the solanums, but take cuttings in case the winter is severe.**

Left: Orange and yellow tropaeolums give hot splashes of color in the foreground. They are backed by a soothing white planting and large, floppy-leaved daturas.

Below: If there is not enough space for a tall runabout member of the *Tropaeolum* family, try the dwarf annual, 'Empress of India'.

Opposite page, above: *Tropaeolum speciosum* dislikes hot, dry gardens. Cool, moist conditions are vital if your garden is to be enriched by its scarlet flowers.

Opposite page, below: The ever-popular, tropical African *Thunbergia alata* is better known as black-eyed Susan.

The rhizomatous *Tropaeolum speciosum* grows 10 ft (3 m) high, producing scarlet flowers followed by bright blue berries. It needs a cool, moist garden. Where severe frosts occur, dig up the rhizomes, taking care not to damage them, and store them in a dry, cool but frost-free place over winter. *T. ciliatum* demands similar conditions, but is slightly shorter with old-gold flowers veined red at the center; one added bonus is that it is evergreen in mild winters. The big favorite, the orange, free-flowering, sun-loving *T. tuberosum* var. *lineamaculatum* 'Ken Aslet' is more tender than those mentioned above, so where temperatures fall below freezing bring it indoors to overwinter, or in mild areas give it a deep protective mulch.

The annual nasturtiums (*Tropaeolum majus*) have the edge over the perennials in terms of popularity and sheer ease of cultivation—simply pop in the large, easy-to handle seeds in sunny spots where they are to grow and remember to water regularly. In the garden of the Impressionist painter, Monet, in Giverny, north of Paris, you can see them at their most spectacular and be inspired. The approach to Monet's front door, known as the Grande Allée, is a 15 ft (5 m) wide gravel path. Along the path, at intervals of about 15 ft (5 m), there are tall metal arches covered in glorious climbing roses. Annual nasturtiums line the edges of the sun-drenched path, soon creeping across it and smothering the walkway in an exuberant riot of green foliage

Use easy-to-grow annual nasturtiums to create a riot of vivid color.

and vivid red flowers. The same idea may be imitated in any garden, perhaps trailing the nasturtiums around a pond or a plinth, or up and over small hoops in the ground; alternatively, grow them up over a 8 ft (2.5 m) high arbor.

Finally, a rare but marvelous scrambling climber is the 10 ft (3 m) high perennial *Caiophora lateritia* from South America. Its five-petaled flowers are the color of ripe peaches and are reminiscent of an open rose; they are followed in the fall by spiraling, twisted seed pods. Grow it over shrubs and provide a thick winter mulch against frosts. The leaves are hairy with stinging bristles, so avoid it if you have children.

Grow vigorous summer-flowering climbers in white or exuberant colors to add interest to vertical surfaces such as walls and trees.

Summer blockbusters

There are two particularly vigorous summer climbers, both of which are deciduous and produce white flowers: the climbing hydrangea (*Hydrangea petiolaris*) and *Schizophragma integrifolium*. Both cling by aerial roots and can easily exceed 40 ft (12 m). *Hydrangea petiolaris* is quite happy on walls that receive little sun, or clambering up a solid, mature tree. It is a big, beefy grower, but takes several years to get going. The flowers last only two to three weeks in the summer, and the dark green leaves turn yellow in the autumn, before falling. Cut plants back in spring.

Schizophragma integrifolium has a longer flowering period of two months, but the flowers can be checked by late spring frosts. Grow it against a wall, with pale green box (*Buxus*) balls in a row at the base, and surrounded by spring tulips and blue agapanthus. A good climber to grow through *Schizophragma integrifolium* is the Chilean glory flower (*Eccremocarpus scaber*). It can reach 12 ft (4 m) in a season and produces bright orange flowers all summer and into fall. The Anglia Hybrids come in bright, brash colors from pink to orange. In areas with mild winters, this plant can be grown as a perennial. In colder areas, it is best treated as an annual.

Above right: **A well-known "blockbuster,"** *Hydrangea petiolaris* **has a big following. However, its flowers are not as long lasting as those of** *Schizophragma integrifolium.*

Opposite page, above: **The long-flowering** *Schizophragma integrifolium* **has creamy bracts that surround the tiny flowers. These turn pink before fading to beige.**

Summer climbers with exotic appeal

There are numerous summer climbers that are exotic in appearance, yet are easy to grow, even in areas with harsh winters. The South American blue passion flower (*Passiflora caerulea*), with its extraordinary, intricate, and elaborate blue and white flowers, is much hardier than it looks: even when its top-growth gets zapped by frosts, new shoots appear the following spring.

Climbers with exotic-looking flowers can be surprisingly easy to grow even in cool areas, although some are best grown in a pot and moved under glass in winter.

It reaches up to 20 ft (6 m) high, and the summer to early-autumn flowers are followed by exotic bright orange fruit. Two excellent alternatives include the white and pale lilac *P. incarnata* and the white and pink *P. lutea*. Both grow to about 6½ ft (2 m) high and are fully hardy, tolerating temperatures as low as −4°F (−20°C), although the recommended minimum is 20°F (−8°C). In warm summers, *P. incarnata* produces edible fruit, more reliably if the plant is grown in a pot and taken inside under glass for the winter months. All passion flowers prefer to be grown on sunny, sheltered walls.

Left: **The flamboyant *Passiflora caerulea* is so striking and quirky that finding the right place for it in the garden can be tricky, as it may not combine well with other climbers. The best solution is to grow it on its own, such as scrambling through this bench.**

Make the most of a warm, sheltered wall by growing exotic and vibrantly colored flowering climbers over it to give your garden or patio a tropical look.

Campsis × *tagliabuana* 'Madame Galen', from the Southeast, is equally exotic-looking and hardy. It is a magnificent climber, with rampant growth, at least 25 ft (8 m) high, with striking orange-red, tubular flowers that are 2½–3 in (6–8 cm) long, and almost as wide. Given warm summers and a sunny wall, it should thrive and flourish. Avoid other trumpet creepers (*Campsis*) unless you live in a very mild area or have a large conservatory, in which case you can grow them in pots.

Spectacular and unusual, the Mexican *Rhodochiton atrosanguineus* is also easy to grow. It can reach 10 ft (3 m) and produces fabulous deep purple, downward-facing, bell-shaped flowers with a protruding vertical purple-black corolla. The flowers, which keep appearing until the frosts, are followed by rounded capsules full of seeds. Save the seed when ripe and keep it in a cool, dry place over winter for sowing next year. Train these plants against a warm wall with wires, or an easier option is to grow them in pots with a frame to climb up.

Aristolochia macrophylla is often called the Dutchman's pipe, owing to its wonderfully bizarre, mottled green, curved flowers, thin at one end and bulbous at the other. Its kidneylike, deciduous leaves are 8 in (20 cm) long. It is a frost-hardy vigorous twining climber, reaching 20 ft (6 m), and requires sun and shelter: grow it over an arbor, where its flowers may be best enjoyed. Little pruning is required beyond removing weak or damaged growth in summer after flowering.

Above left: *Aristolochia manshuriensis* can grow 45 ft (12 m) high. It has larger leaves and flowers than *A. macrophylla* and is far superior, but very rare.

Right: **From mountainous southern Mexico, *Rhodochiton atrosanguineus* is an easily grown annual with appealing flowers. The stems need support from stakes or wires.**

Above right and opposite page: **In late summer and fall, *Campsis* × *tagliabuana* 'Madame Galen' produces vivid orange-red flowers. Grow it on a sunny wall.**

Autumn-flowering clematis

Numerous clematis flower into autumn (*all Group 3, see page 76*), many offering fabulous, decorative seedheads as well as single or double flowers in a variety of shapes. For autumn flowers, *Clematis* 'Huldine', 15 ft (5 m) high, is hard to beat, with its white petals with mauve undersides: to get a good view of it, grow it up and over a sunny wall, to allow you to see through the near-translucent blooms. Other excellent autumn-flowerers include the white *C. chinensis*, 12 ft (4 m) high, and the primrose-yellow *C. connata*, 15 ft (5 m) high. *C.* 'Lady Betty Balfour' is a gorgeous purple-blue, reaching 10 ft (3 m) high. *C. flammula* 'Sieboldii' starts off pale white and turns pale green. It is an intriguing climber, slightly resembling a passion flower, but is extremely difficult to grow.

For decorative seedheads, opt for the large, colorful *Clematis* 'Bill MacKenzie', which grows to 20 ft (6 m), and can smother a long stretch of wall or neighboring plants with its bright yellow flowers and wispy, silky gray seedheads. The less vigorous *C. aethusifolia*, 6½ ft (2 m) high, also produces both yellow flowers and attractive seedheads. In larger gardens, try *C. vitalba*, commonly called old man's beard. It reaches a massive, sprawling 30 ft (10 m), and is covered in white flowers and silver-gray seedheads in late fall and early winter.

Left: **Its leaves are coarse, but when the late-flowering *Clematis* × *jouiniana* is in full bloom they are obscured by the mass of starry white flowers. Alternatively, grow the cultivar *C.* × *j.* 'Praecox', which starts flowering about eight weeks earlier.**

Below right: ***Clematis* 'Abundance' produces plentiful crimson blooms over a long flowering period from late summer to fall.**

Autumn-flowering climbers

The choice of climbers that perform right at the end of the season is quite small. However, there are still several good clematis with attractive, fluffy seedheads, and roses with colorful orange-red or scarlet hips. *Celastrus orbiculatus* in full berry is also a gorgeous sight. It has early summer green flowers, followed by pea-size yellow fruit with scarlet seeds inside that last for several weeks. You need either the hermaphrodite form or both male and female plants in order for the plants to produce fruit. *C. orbiculatus* is a vigorous 40 ft (12 m) grower and makes a twining tangle that looks sensational combined with an ivy in full berry. Grow it in a cottage garden, where it can zigzag at will, rather than in a formal planting. It needs fertile and free draining soil to thrive.

If you want to use clematis as ground cover, a good choice is the pale blue *Clematis × jouiniana*, which sprawls across 25 ft (8 m), given humus-rich, fertile soil. It looks very effective twining through herbaceous perennials in the bed. If you prefer, it can also be tied and trained to a wall. Its cultivar *C. × jouiniana* 'Praecox' starts flowering slightly earlier, at the end of summer, but grows to only half the height.

Left: **The large silvery seedheads of** *Clematis* **'Bill MacKenzie' sparkle in the sunshine. They prolong the season of interest once flowering is over.**

Above: *Clematis* **'Huldine' blooms from late summer to fall. It looks wonderful forming a canopy of blossom, beneath which light glimmers through the flowers.**

Left: *Rosa* 'Paul's Himalayan Musk' flowers once, in mid-summer, for about three weeks. Until then, it gives no hint of the impressive display it will produce. Its stems snake up the host—here a silver birch—developing thousands of buds. These open into masses of pink blooms followed by hips.

Opposite page, right: *Rosa* 'Iceberg, Climbing' looks delightful growing into a cherry tree. The combination gives fresh white flowers from spring to the first frost.

Opposite page, below left: *Rosa* 'Arthur Bell' is the climbing sport of the award-winning floribunda. It grows 11½ ft (3.5 m) high, flowering into fall. The yellow blooms age to rich cream.

Opposite page, below center: The small hips of *Rosa* 'Francis E. Lester' follow its white flowers and pink buds. The flowers smell like a mixture of bananas and oranges.

Opposite page, below right: *Rosa* 'Highfield' has creamy flowers through to the end of the season.

Late-season roses

Many climbing roses, unlike the ramblers, repeat flower from summer into the fall. The yellow *Rosa* 'Arthur Bell, Climbing', pale yellow *R.* 'Highfield', light pink *R.* 'New Dawn', and pink *R.* 'Dream Girl', all 10 ft (3 m) high, are just a few of those climbers that add color from summer through to the first frosts.

Most roses also provide plenty of brightly colored berries or hips. Although they are on display from midsummer, the hips are particularly welcome in late autumn, when there is less competition from other plants. The best hips are on *Rosa rugosa* and its cultivars, about 6–8 ft (1.8–2.5 m) high, as well as on several wild roses and their hybrids, such as *R. macrophylla* 'Master Hugh', of about the same height.

A selection of small-hipped roses includes *Rosa* 'Bobbie James', *R.* 'Kew Rambler', and *R.* 'Paul's Himalayan Musk', all to 30 ft (10 m), and *R.* 'Frances E. Lester', to 15 ft (5 m). *R. helenae* and *R. polyantha grandiflora*, both reaching 20 ft (6 m), have medium-size hips. For larger hips, choose *R.* 'Allen Chandler', 10 ft (3 m) high, in pink, or *R.* 'Cupid', 15 ft (5 m) high, in peach.

Hips combine beautifully with mauve sweet peas to lift a purple border, and also with the red-purple foliage of *Cotinus coggygria* 'Royal Purple', or the yellow-margined leaves of *Aralia elata* 'Aureovariegata', a form of the Japanese angelica tree. The adventurous gardener can plant vibrant red and orange crocosmias beneath the roses to provide an echoing accent of strong color around the base.

FLOWERS GALLERY

gallery flowers

Campsis × tagliabuana 'Madame Galen' (Trumpet creeper)

Height: 25 ft (8 m); flowers: late summer to autumn; fully hardy

Deciduous aerial-root climber with elegant, exotic-looking, slender, trumpet-shaped, orange-red flowers. Requires full sun and fertile, moist but well-drained soil; provide thick spring and fall mulches. Grow the plant up a wall, fence, or tree.

Pruning: In spring, reduce sideshoots by 2 in (5 cm) to within three to four buds of the main stem to restrict growth.

Eccremocarpus scaber (Chilean glory flower)

Height: 12 ft (4 m); leaves: year-round; flowers: late spring to autumn; frost hardy

Evergreen, fast-growing tendril climber. Produces showy orange flowers. Requires fertile, well-drained soil in full sun. In cold areas, grow as an annual from seed in late winter at 61°F (16°C). A good climber for scrambling over or through other shrubs or for growing over a garden structure.

Pruning: Cut back growth in fall, leaving a small covering as frost protection. Replace with new cuttings every few years in spring.

Hydrangea petiolaris (Climbing hydrangea)

Height: 40 ft (12 m), or more in favorable conditions; flowers: summer; fully hardy

Sturdy, deciduous aerial-root climber with 4 in (10 cm) long leaves with heart-shaped bases and white flowers. Requires fertile, moist but well-drained soil; mulch in spring and summer. Needs a stout structure for support, such as a wall or large, mature tree.

Pruning: Cut back shoots in spring to restrict growth for the available space.

Passiflora caerulea (Blue passion flower)

Height: 20 ft (6 m); leaves: year-round; flowers: summer to autumn; fruits: autumn; frost hardy

Evergreen tendril climber that has spectacular white flowers with blue and purple markings, and yellow fruit. Requires fertile, well-drained soil in full sun. Grow against a wall, or on an arbor.

Pruning: After flowering, prune shoots to within three buds. Remove any spindly or dead growth as needed.

Schizophragma integrifolium

Height: 40 ft (12 m); flowers: summer; frost hardy

Deciduous, aerial-root climber with small, slightly scented creamy white flowers, gently fading to pink. The dark green foliage acts as an effective foil to the flowers. Needs humus-rich, moist but well-drained soil to thrive. Can grow in sun or partial shade. Best grown up a strong, preferably sunny, wall or into a mature tree.

Pruning: Little required and dislikes excessive cutting back.

Solanum crispum (Chilean potato tree)

Height: 20 ft (6 m); leaves: year-round in mild winters; flowers: summer; frost hardy

Evergreen or semievergreen (may lose its leaves in cold winters). A scrambling climber producing a prolific display of fragrant lilac or dark purple-blue flowers followed by cream-colored fruit. Requires fertile, well-drained soil in full sun to thrive; add a protective spring and summer mulch around the base of the plant. Grow it up around other climbers, or train the shoots on lengths of wire secured at intervals along a wall.

Pruning: Remove spindly or dead growth in spring. Cut back any old unproductive stems to the ground after flowering to force new vigorous growth to occur.

Tropaeolum tuberosum var. *lineamaculatum* 'Ken Aslet'

Height: 8 ft (2.5 m); flowers: midsummer to autumn; half hardy

Perennial scrambling climber—the most popular *Tropaeolum* cultivar—producing vibrant orange flowers over a long season. Requires moist but well-drained soil in a bright place. Water frequently during the growing period. Lift the tubers in the fall and keep them in a dry, frost-free place for replanting the following spring.

Pruning: None required.

Above left: **Campsis** × **tagliabuana 'Madame Galen'**

Above right: **Hydrangea petiolaris**

Left: **Passiflora caerulea**

Right: **Passiflora caerulea racemosa**

Below left: **Solanum crispum 'Glasnevin'**

Left: **Eccremocarpus scaber**

Opposite page: **Rosa 'Arthur Bell'**

Some flowering climbers that will not survive outside all year round can be grown in containers in a sunroom and brought outdoors when the weather warms up. This way, you can add a tropical feel to your garden in summer with, say, pots of bougainvillea on a sunny patio.

TENDER

Tender climbers usually benefit from a spell outdoors during the warm months and can make striking seasonal features.

Numerous climbers are frost tender or half hardy, and will not survive outdoors in a frost-prone climate over winter; however, many of the most popular types will grow happily in containers in a solarium. Bring the pots outside into the yard in summer and take them indoors before the first frosts. The plants usually benefit from a spell outdoors and can make striking seasonal features—for example, imagine potted bougainvilleas in a garden of mirrors and patterned tiles; the large red and yellow flowers of *Gloriosa superba* 'Rothschildiana' growing up stakes among lettuces; or a scented hoya inside a hot, sunny porch. Below is a selection of tender climbers; there are others, too, not described here, that also require high levels of humidity.

Bougainvilleas are grown for their amazing, brightly colored, papery bracts surrounding one or three tiny, star-shaped flowers.

Potted climbers will not reach their maximum height, as the pot restricts their root run, but they still need to be kept in check. Most can be pruned lightly in autumn and more heavily in spring. If they become too big, discard them and replace them with a cutting.

The heights of the potted climbers given throughout this chapter indicate the maximum size that the plants will reach when grown in a 12 in (30 cm) container.

Flowering tender climbers

Among the most amazing of the tender climbers are the bougainvilleas, which sometimes grow up to 10 ft (3 m) in a pot, but can easily be pruned to restrict their size. Their blooms are not actually flowers, but brightly colored papery bracts in shades of red, pink, orange, and white, which surround the one or three tiny, star-shaped true flowers held in the center of each bract. Be careful when handling bougainvilleas: they climbs using vicious thorns. *Plumbago auriculata* is another tender climber of great merit. The species is available in just one color, a beautiful, soft pale blue, but there is also a white form *(P. a.* var. *alba)*. Both produce generous clusters of slender-tubed flowers, and can grow 15 ft (5 m) high, or 5 ft (1.5 m) in a pot, but will withstand hard pruning in spring and winter to keep growth in check. They prefer temperatures of around 45°F (7°C). Water plumbagos plentifully and feed monthly with a liquid fertilizer during the growing season; water sparingly in the winter. Several pots of *P. auriculata* look particularly good clustered around a pond.

Few climbers are more dramatic looking than the tuberous *Gloriosa superba* 'Rothschildiana', with its startling, elaborate, bright red and yellow butterflylike flowers. Despite its exotic appearance, it is easier to grow than you might think. If you live in a cool climate, plant it up in spring under glass, increase the temperature gradually to 50°F (10°C), then move it outside to a sunny position when the weather becomes warm. As soon as any growth appears, water the plant regularly and feed it with liquid fertilizer every two weeks. It grows about 6 ft (1.8 m) high.

Far left: **The tuberous *Gloriosa superba* 'Rothschildiana' looks too exotic for cool climates, but just needs a kick start in spring in a heated propagator.**

Center: **Bougainvillea, named after admiral Louis Antoine, Comte de Bougainville,** 1729–1811, the first Frenchman to cross the Pacific, is so magnificent that it rarely needs companions. However, a richly colored *Ipomoea* twining through it would look very effective.

Left: **The flowers of *Plumbago auriculata*—a lovely pale blue.**

Scented tender climbers

There are many scented climbers, among them *Dregea sinensis*, with its beautiful small, star-shaped white flowers with pink speckling, which reaches 10 ft (3 m) high or 7 ft (2.2 m) in a pot. It can tolerate frost, but is best kept at a minimum temperature of 45°F (7°C) over winter. It can survive outside all year in mild gardens, but needs a warm, sheltered position and a protective mulch. Grow it up a frame of wires, or let it weave over shrubs.

Hoya australis, *H. carnosa,* and *H. globulosa* all present their waxy, star-shaped flowers in showy, rounded clusters. *H. australis* has white flowers with a decorative red spot at the base of each petal and grows about 15 ft (5 m) high. It needs a minimum winter temperature of 50°F (10°C). *H. carnosa* and *H. globulosa* are about the same height, but are slightly hardier, surviving at 41–45°F (5–7°C). *H. carnosa* has pure white flowers, doubles as a trailing plant, and can be grown in a hanging basket, while *H. globulosa* has furry stems. All three need moderate humidity in summer in order to thrive. The best place to grow them apart from the sunroom is in a bright, sunny, well-ventilated porch: place the pots on trays filled with pebbles and water, or mist the growth with a hand spray twice a day. Use a good potting medium, with added grit for fast drainage, water plentifully and feed monthly during the growing season. Keep the plants cool in winter and do not let the soil dry out. Either prune in spring or after flowering to restrict the plant's size, but avoid cutting back hard.

One of the most gloriously scented, and popular, of all flowering climbers is jasmine. The easiest-to-grow, hardiest jasmine for the garden is *Jasminum officinale* (see page 21), but there are also several highly ornamental kinds that require mild winters or the protection of a heated, enclosed porch or conservatory. *J. grandiflorum* has slightly larger flowers—about 1½ in (4 cm) wide—than *J. officinale* and needs a minimum winter temperature of 45°F (7°C).

Jasminum polyanthum is the indoor pot plant commonly sold in garden centers. Keep its growth in check by pruning and thinning after flowering, possibly reducing old woody stems to within 4 in (10 cm) of the soil. Stand the plant outside in the summer in dappled shade, give it a potash-high feed, never let the soil dry out, and bring it back indoors in the fall. The Indian *J. sambac* has the largest flowers of all the jasmines, 2 in (5 cm) wide, but is also one of the most tender, preferring a minimum temperature of about 61°F (16°C).

Top left: **For a jasmine with a large flower, grow *Jasminum sambac*. It should keep flowering on and off over winter if brought indoors and kept in a warm room.**

Above: **The scent of the hoya-like Chinese evergreen *Dregea sinensis* is like honey.**

Right: ***Hoya australis* is named after Thomas Hoy, a 19th-century gardener at Syon House, London. It needs good humidity to thrive.**

Far right: **The scent of *Jasminum polyanthum* is almost overwhelming. Plants do best outside in summer.**

Hoya australis, *H. carnosa,* and *H. globulosa* all present their waxy, star-shaped flowers in showy, rounded

clusters. *H. australis* has white flowers with a decorative red spot at the base of each petal and reaches 15 ft (5 m).

Fruiting tender climbers

Some frost-tender *Passiflora* species and cultivars produce sweet, edible fruit. In cold climates, they may be grown inside in pots over winter at a minimum temperature of 40°F (4°C), but preferably at about 50°F (10°C). *Passiflora edulis*, which produces the commercial passion fruit, has elaborately structured, exotic-looking white, green, and purple flowers. The 2 in (5 cm) long fruit continues to ripen through the fall and into early winter; then it turns purple and eventually drops. Continue watering to keep the soil moist up to this stage, but do not let the roots become waterlogged. The chief autumn and winter requirement for *Passiflora* species is bright sunlight. Although the plants are self-pollinating, hand-pollination increases the yield.

Passiflora species may also be grown in a heated bed in a greenhouse. Thread the growing stem out through a small hole in the wall, filling the gaps to prevent any drafts, so the growth occurs outside. *P. vitifolia*, which produces startling, swept-back crimson flowers, 6 in (15 cm) across, and striking bronze new

Top left: **There are scores of excellent passifloras to choose from, and new hybrids keep appearing. *Passiflora vitifolia* has startling red flowers.**

Left: ***Passiflora × violacea* has showy flowers from mid-spring to late fall.**

Above: ***Passiflora edulis* produces sweet edible fruit.**

foliage, is ideal for this method. Place it near the door so it receives plenty of fresh air in summer and provide a heated bed of 45°F (7°C) in winter. In mild weather, it may flower from mid-spring until early winter. It needs pollinating with *P. caerulea*: just transfer the pollen with a paintbrush.

Hardier plants

Some climbers are borderline hardy plants that may survive a mild winter outside if they are given a protective mulch in early fall or winter to insulate the roots. *Dregea sinensis* (*see page 66*) fits into this category, as do two other climbers: the Australian *Billardiera longiflora* and the Chilean *Lapageria rosea*.

Billardiera longiflora, which grows to 10 ft (3 m) in the ground or 6½ ft (2 m) in a pot, produces highly ornamental but inedible, fleshy, purple-blue fruits that follow its flowers; its pale green summer flowers are relatively insignificant. It can be grown outside against a sheltered, sunny wall in lime-free soil, provided the winter temperature does not dip much below freezing, although 45°F (7°C) is safer. They dislike bright sun; the dappled shade of other shrubs and trees is ideal.

Lapageria rosea, the national flower of Chile, has fabulous, 3½ in (9 cm) long waxy red flowers, on 12 ft (4 m) long stems in a bed, or 6 ft (1.8 m) long stems in a pot. It will tolerate temperatures as low as 23°F (−5°C), although 32–45°F (0–7°C) is a safer minimum, and requires light, cool shade in a moist, lime-free soil as well as the protection of a wall.

Below: **The Australian** *Billardiera longiflora*, **the climbing blueberry, forms a mass of growth, 10 ft (3 m) high. The twining, woody stems become covered with purple berries. As with many tender climbers, take cuttings and start again when the plant gets out of hand. This plant is not fussy and ought to be more widely grown.** *B. scandens* **grows up to 5 ft (1.5 m) higher.**

TENDER GALLERY

Billardiera longiflora
(Climbing blueberry)

Height: 10 ft (3 m) in the ground or 6½ ft (2 m) in a pot; leaves: year-round; flowers: summer; fruit: autumn; frost hardy, but prefers a minimum temperature of 45°F (7°C)

Evergreen twining climber grown mainly for its very attractive, globular purple fruits that follows yellow flowers. Keep the roots and pot in shade, and the top-growth out of scorching sunlight. In frost-prone areas, grow under glass in bright, filtered light. In a pot, use an ericaceous (lime-free) medium. Water sparingly in winter, and in late winter pot on or top-dress. If growing outdoors in a mild climate, plants need humus-rich, moist but well-drained, lime-free soil. Keep well watered and feed monthly with liquid fertilizer from spring through to fall. Grow against a house wall or over an arbor, or allow to scramble through sturdy shrubs.
Pruning: After flowering, thin out old shoots as required and, if it becomes necessary, trim shoots to restrict the size of the plant to suit the available space.

Bougainvillea cultivars

Height: 8–10 ft (2.5–3 m) in a pot; leaves: year-round; floral bracts: mainly from summer to autumn; half-hardy to frost tender

Evergreen scrambling climbers grown for the flamboyant colors—rich and pale reds, pinks, oranges, and white—of the petallike bracts that surround their small, tubular flowers. In a pot, use equal quantities of potting mix and peat substitute. Plants need a high-nitrogen feed when in growth, and a high-potash feed when in bud; keep the soil just moist when the plants are dormant. Pot on or top-dress pot-grown plants in late winter. Given plenty of light, they may come into flower in a sunroom over winter. In an indoor pot, grow bougainvillea up a bamboo frame. Outdoors, bougainvillea requires fertile, well-drained soil. Grow up an arch or arbor, or against a house wall in full sun. To grow bougainvillea outdoors, choose one of the following: *Bougainvillea × buttiana*, *Bougainvillea glabra,* or *Bougainvillea spectablilis*. These may survive short cold spells with temperatures down to 32°F (0°C) during the winter months as long as the soil around them is kept fairly dry.
Pruning: Prune sideshoots to within three or four buds of the main stem in early spring; vigorous plants that have outgrown their space may also be trimmed in the fall.

Dregea sinensis

Height: 10 ft (3 m) in the ground or 7 ft (2.2 m) in a pot; flowers: summer; frost hardy, but prefers a minimum temperature of 45°F (7°C)

Deciduous twining climber producing highly scented creamy white flowers up to ½ in (1.5 cm) across with pale pink insides that are speckled scarlet. The flowers are followed by slim seedpods. To grow in a pot, use potting medium with added grit to improve drainage. Water frequently in summer. Outdoors, grow in fertile, well-drained soil, in sun or dappled shade.
Pruning: Cut back the sideshoots in spring to restrict the plant's size. (It is recommended that you wear gloves to do this, since they leak a very sticky sap.)

Gloriosa superba
'Rothschildiana'

Height: about 6½ ft (2 m) in a pot; flowers: summer to autumn; frost tender—withstands a minimum temperature of 46–50°F (8–10°C)

Twining climber producing exotic, elegant, scarlet flowers, with striking contrasting yellow coloring on the bases and around their margins. The flowers deepen in color as they fade. In a pot, plant the tuber 4 in (10 cm) deep in a good potting medium, with added grit to improve drainage. Reduce watering in the fall as the tuber dies back. Keep over winter in a cool, frost-free place. Outdoors, grow in fertile, well-drained soil in full sun. It looks most effective when allowed to scramble through other plants and can be used to extend the season of interest of a spring-flowering shrub whose blooms are over. In frost-prone areas, keep the plant in its container so it can be easily moved back indoors under glass during the winter months.
Pruning: If necessary, cut back shoots to restrict the plant's size.

Far left:
Bougainvillea glabra

Left:
Dregea sinensis

Center:
Jasminum polyanthum

Below left:
Gloriosa superba 'Rothschildiana'

Below center:
Lapageria rosea

Below:
Billardiera longiflora

Opposite page:
Jasminum polyanthum

Jasminum polyanthum
(Jasmine)

Height: 10 ft (3 m) or more in the border or 4 ft (1.2 m) in a pot: leaves: year-round; flowers: late winter or early spring in a warm conservatory, or from spring through to summer outdoors in a warm climate; half hardy

Evergreen twining climber with huge sprays of white, highly scented flowers. In a pot, use a good potting medium. Water sparingly in winter. Outdoors, plants prefer fertile, well-drained soil in dappled shade or sun.
Pruning: After flowering, reduce flowering shoots to promote vigorous side-growth.

Lapageria rosea
(Chilean bellflower)

Height: 12 ft (4 m) in the border or 6 ft (1.8 m) in a pot; leaves: year-round; flowers: summer to late autumn; half hardy

Evergreen twining climber bearing exotic red flowers. In a pot, needs ericaceous (lime-free) potting medium with added sharp sand. Outdoors, requires moist but well-drained soil and plenty of leaf mold. Needs a cool, partially shaded site in summer.
Pruning: Cut back shoots lightly to restrict the plant's size for the available space.

Passiflora edulis
(Passion fruit)

Height: 12 ft (4 m) in the border or 6 ft (1.8 m) in a pot; leaves: year-round; flowers: summer; fruit: follows flowers in late summer to early fall; frost tender

Evergreen tendril climber with eye-catching flowers and edible fruit. In a pot, needs potting medium, with plenty of added grit for drainage. Once buds form, feed with tomato fertilizer. Outdoors, grow in fertile, moist but well-drained soil in full sun or partial shade. Dislikes cold, wet soil over winter. Also, beware of over-potting, over-watering, and over-feeding, all quite common causes of plants failing to flourish.
Pruning: After flowering, prune shoots to within three buds. Remove any spindly or dead growth. Remove top-growth.

Plumbago auriculata
(Cape leadwort)

Height: 15 ft (5 m) in the ground or 5 ft (1.5 m) in a pot; leaves: year-round; flowers: summer to late autumn; half hardy

Evergreen scrambling climber with gorgeous pale blue flowers. In a pot, grow in potting medium lightened with sand and peat substitute. Keep over winter at 45°F (7°C). Outdoors, needs fertile, well-drained soil.
Pruning: Hard prune last year's flowering stems in early spring.

Rhodochiton atrosanguineus

Height: 10 ft (3 m); flowers: summer to autumn; frost tender

Deciduous twining climber with black to rosy purple pendant, bell-shaped flowers. Grow from seed each spring at 61°F (16°C) in light conditions, but with some protection from scorching sunlight. Plant in a pot filled with potting medium or, when hardened off to outside temperatures, against a sheltered, sunny wall in moist but well-drained, humus-rich soil. In mild areas, it looks particularly splendid when trained over an arch or arbor.
Pruning: None required, but pinch out tips to encourage new growth.

Right: **Plumbago auriculata**

care and cultivation

Climbers bring an attractive vertical element to the garden. They can clamber up walls and fences, scramble through other plants, or weave their way around attractive garden structures such as trellis, pillars, and arbors. Because climbing plants make the most of otherwise wasted space, even the smallest plot has room for a climber.

Choosing climbers

Before you choose a climber, first make sure your yard can accommodate its mature dimensions. If you have a small courtyard, a large climber such as *Hydrangea petiolaris*, with its sturdy trunk, may take over your limited space. However, this does not mean that larger climbers are unsuitable for those with smaller yards. While some potentially large plants such as wisteria can reach 46 ft (14 m) if left alone, its annual pruning regime, which promotes more flowers, can restrict its height by one-third. Growing a climber in a container, or training it into a weeping standard, also means that its height will be restricted.

It is also important to make sure the supporting frame will be able to bear the eventual weight and height of the mature climber. Some climbers, such as sweet peas (*Lathyrus odoratus*), will be happy with a light wigwam constructed from twigs or sticks, while others, such as wisteria, require a strong, stout support—a house wall or a sturdy wooden structure.

Climbing plants are usually sold in containers, although some species (such as climbing roses) may be sold as bare-root specimens. Always select a healthy-looking plant with an attractive outline and plenty of healthy leaves and shoots. Bare-root climbers should have sturdy, well-developed, fibrous roots.

Planting and training

Planting against a wall

Since the soil at the foot of a wall can be relatively dry and impoverished, position the planting hole at least 12–18 in (30–45 cm) away from the base of the wall, where the soil will be better and the plant will receive more rain. The hole should be at least twice the diameter of the climber's container.

Hungry climbers such as roses need fertile soil, so prepare the ground before planting by removing any weeds and digging in plenty of well-rotted manure or potting medium. Plunge the potted rootball in a bucket of water for 15 minutes, until the soil is saturated, then leave it to drain for 30 minutes to one hour.

Invert the pot carefully, supporting the top of the plant, then slide the rootball out of the pot. Plant the climber at the same depth as in its original pot. Clematis are the exception to this rule – they must be planted 2½ in (6 cm) below the soil surface, where potential replacement buds form, ready to grow if the top-growth is damaged or if clematis wilt strikes.

Angle the stem toward the wall at a 45° angle, along a stake if necessary, and disentangle the roots, spreading them toward the open ground. Fill in around the plant, then firm down the soil. If planting during a dry spell, water well, especially during spring and summer. A spring mulch, 3 in (7 cm) deep, will help thwart weeds and prevent moisture evaporation.

Most climbers, except those such as ivy (*Hedera*) and Virginia creeper (*Parthenocissus*), which climb using sticky pads, will need to be tied to a support attached to the wall, or trained onto a frame of horizontal wires. To construct a frame, use strong, galvanized wire. Attach it to vine eyes drilled into the wall, or to trellis attached to the wall. Keep the wire 2¾ in (7 cm) away from the surface to provide good air circulation. The horizontal wires should be about 16 in (40 cm) apart. In the case of a lightweight annual climber such as *Rhodochiton atrosanguineus*, a ready-made trellis, screwed to wooden strips attached to the wall, is fine.

Trees and shrubs as supports

Climbers adjacent to trees and hedges also need enriched planting holes and regular watering, but should be planted at least 3 ft (90 cm) away from their host plant, as the two will be competing for food and water. Position a stake between the two plants so the climber can scramble along to the tree or shrub. Wait until trees are well established before using them as hosts, and plant the climber in the face of the prevailing wind, so that it is blown into its support, not away from it. Grow annual or herbaceous climbers on hedges and shrubs that need fall or spring clipping; otherwise, access is difficult.

Wigwams and lightweight metal frames

Roses, clematis, and lightweight climbing annuals such as sweet peas can all be

Planting container climbers against a wall Position the planting hole at least 12–18 in (30–45 cm) away from the wall.

Gently disentangle the roots, spreading them out so they face away from the wall.

Choosing climbers Avoid plants whose roots are coiled around the root ball or are dangling through the drainage holes.

trained up bamboo wigwams or lightweight obelisks. The enriched planting hole for permanent shrubs can be larger than those close to a wall, up to 3 feet square (1 metre square). The tendril climbers, such as clematis, will need initial tying in, but thereafter will clamber happily over the structure. Horticultural string wrapped around the support will give the climber an added leg-up. Training the climber around its support, in flattish, near-horizontal layers, will promote plenty of flowering vertical side shoots. Most climbers, particularly clematis, prefer their roots in the shade, and their top-growth in the sun.

Ornamental structures

Heavy, rampant growth requires the strong support of sturdy wooden or metal structures such as arbors, bowers, and arches. Attach wires for tying in. Train growth up each support (and along any horizontals), then across the roof. By spiralling growth around supports, many more flowering shoots will appear low down, but the growth will take longer to cover the top.

Climbers in pots

Use sturdy terracotta pots that will not be blown over. Always fill the base with plastic chips or small stones to facilitate drainage. Since new potting medium quickly loses its nutrients, for a good flower display feed with a tomato fertilizer once buds appear. In subsequent years, either repot or replace the top layer of soil and add a slow-release fertilizer. Water climbers in pots regularly, especially in hot, dry weather. When the roots poke through the drainage holes, pot up to the next size container. If a climber grows too large for its position, take cuttings and start again, or root-prune by cutting back the root system and the top-growth by about one-third in spring.

Combining climbers

When choosing several climbers for the same structure, it is important to make sure that they require similar growing conditions, that one will not swamp the other, and that there is no danger of two with very different pruning needs becoming entwined. For an impressive eight-month display, try combining spring clematis and wisteria on a long sturdy trellis, followed by early-summer clematis, summer roses, and honeysuckle, then late-summer clematis and roses, followed by the rich-purple autumn foliage of *Vitis vinifera* 'Purpurea'.

For a novel display of climbers, try fruit and vegetables (not strictly climbers, but they can be used as such). Apple trees can be trained as cordons to grow over arches and tunnels. You can also create an open sunny tunnel, with latticed wooden sides, for pears, peas, beans, tomatoes, and trailing squash.

Pruning

Most climbers need some routine pruning: it encourages healthy growth and a strong framework, enhances the shape, keeps the size in check, and promotes flowering or fruiting. Routine maintenance may involve removing spent flowers (unless berries form), thinning out crowded shoots, removing spindly or damaged stems, and cutting back to restrict size. Of course, any climbers causing potential damage to roofs, twining around drainpipes, blocking gutters, and dislodging shingles must also be kept under control. Cut them back well before the problem arises.

When and how to prune

The time of year when established climbers are to be pruned depends entirely on their flowering season. Since climbers flowering from spring to midsummer usually do so on the previous year's growth, prune them immediately after flowering, allowing them enough time to produce new shoots before the winter months.

Climbers that flower later in the year usually do so on new growth. These should be pruned in the fall or in early spring before new buds appear. The exceptions to the rule are the berrying or fruiting climbers, which perform after flowering: generally; prune them in spring.

Remove all dead or damaged wood, and cut back weak shoots. Climbers that are outgrowing their allotted space should be chopped back to prevent excessive growth. Always prune stems approximately $1/16$–$1/8$ in (2–4 mm) above a healthy, outward-facing bud, using sharp pruning shears to make a clean, slanting cut.

Pruning clematis

Clematis can be divided into three main pruning groups, based on their flowering time and habit: Group 1 encompasses the early-flowering species and cultivars, which flower in winter and early spring on the previous year's stems; Group 2 is made up of early to mid-season, large-flowered cultivars, which flower in late spring and early summer on the previous year's growth; and Group 3 includes the late cultivars and species, which flower on the current year's shoots in summer and early fall.

Group 1

Many of these vigorous, early-flowering clematis require little, if any, pruning. After flowering, simply prune dead stems, and thin out excessively tangled growth to a new bud. If you remove all the shoots, you will not get any flowers next year.

Group 2

In late winter or early spring, before the onset of the new season's growth, remove dead and damaged stems, and prune back healthy shoots to a strong pair of leaf buds. These buds will produce the first crop of flowers.

Group 3

In early spring, before the new growth appears, cut back all growth to a new bud just above the base of the previous season's growth, approximately 6–12 in (15–30 cm) above ground level.

Pruning roses

The pruning method of roses depends on the type (*see page 77*). Most require initial pruning when planted in the dormant season, or in the first spring if planted in summer. Generally, prune established plants in the fall or early spring.

One-burst flowerers can be pruned immediately after flowering, unless there is a show of hips. With repeat flowerers, remove the spent blooms and cut back to the third bud below to encourage new flowers. In autumn, cut back their flowered shoots by two-thirds, and the main stems to restrict size.

Pruning clematis

Group 1 Clematis Prune any weak or dead stems after flowering, and thin out any excessively tangled growth to a new bud. New growth will ripen during late summer and autumn, and flowers will appear the following spring.

Some examples of Group 1 Clematis:
C. *armandii* 'Apple Blossom'
C. *cirrhosa* 'Freckles'
C. *macropetala* 'Markham's Pink'
C. *macropetala* 'White Swan'
C. *montana* 'Freda'
C. *montana* var. *rubens*

Remove any tangled growth as necessary.

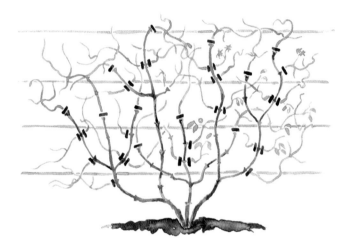

Group 2 Clematis Remove any dead, damaged, or weak stems from these large-flowered cultivars in late winter or early spring before the new season's growth appears. Cut back all the remaining branches to just above a strong pair of leaf buds.

Some examples of Group 2 Clematis:
C. 'Bees' Jubilee'
C. 'Daniel Deronda'
C. 'Gillian Blades'
C. 'Henryi'
C. 'Lasurstern'
C. 'The President'

Prune healthy shoots back to new buds.

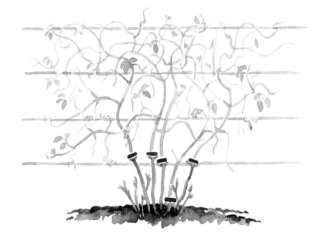

Group 3 Clematis These late-flowering species and cultivars produce flowers on the current season's growth. In early spring, prune all the previous year's stems to just above a pair of strong buds, approximately 6–12 in (15–30 cm) above soil level.

Some examples of Group 3 Clematis:
C. 'Gipsy Queen'
C. 'Jackmanii'
C. 'Mme Edouard André'
C. 'Perle d'Azur
C. 'Victoria'
C. *viticella*

Cut back to a strong pair of leaf buds.

Wall climbers

Do not cut back new climbers at planting if they are to be trained against a wall, or they might revert to smaller bush types. You can, however, nip them back to the next strong bud to encourage plenty of side shoots in spring. Prune established plants annually, according to when they flower (see above). Always cut back to a healthy bud. Clip out any old stems and cut back weak stems to a vigorous shoot. Remove any dead or damaged wood. Where the base of the climber is bare, with all the growth much higher up, cut back the old stems to a height of 12 in (30 cm), but not all in one season.

Arch and arbor climbers

For a wide arch, spread out the shoots to try to cover the full width; on a narrower arch, train the growth up and over the structure. Thereafter, prune as for established wall climbers (above). Against arbors, little pruning is required beyond shortening the flowering shoots in fall or spring.

Tree climbers

It is not necessary to prune roses growing into trees.

Ramblers

If left unpruned, ramblers can become tangled and choked with excess growth. They should be cut back in late summer after flowering. For the first two years, side shoots should be trimmed to a vigorous shoot. After the third year, about a third of the oldest flowering shoots must be cut back to the base of the plant. Tangled, choked ramblers needing renovation can be cut right back. They will quickly recover.

Pruning wisteria

Wisteria have a vigorous habit and require a strict pruning regime initially to create an open structure of branches (and to restrict size in the case of *Wisteria sinensis*); once established, they require a twice-yearly pruning session in midwinter and late summer to promote flowering.

After planting, reduce the main stem to 3 ft (90 cm) above ground level, and remove any side branches. In the first summer, tie in the new side branches or laterals, removing any unwanted ones, to a frame of wires; cut back other shoots to 6–8 in (15–20 cm) to encourage flower-bearing spurs. In the first winter, prune the leading shoot and the lateral or side shoots to two or three buds. This will help strong new branches to form.

In the second summer, pinch out the tip of the leading shoot and cut back thin, spindly side shoots to encourage a bushy habit. In winter, cut back the new lateral growth to two or three buds.

In the third and subsequent years, only routine maintenance pruning is needed. In summer, cut back the lateral growth to within 6 in (15 cm). In winter, prune again to 4 in (10 cm), leaving two or three buds. Check the ties on the main stem each year.

Pests and diseases

Always buy good-quality plants and choose an appropriate soil and site. Avoid planting too close together, since congested plants encourage diseases, and water and feed correctly to promote healthy growth. A regular pruning regime is vital, and diseased or damaged stems should be removed as soon as they occur. Conservatory-grown climbers need plenty of fresh air.

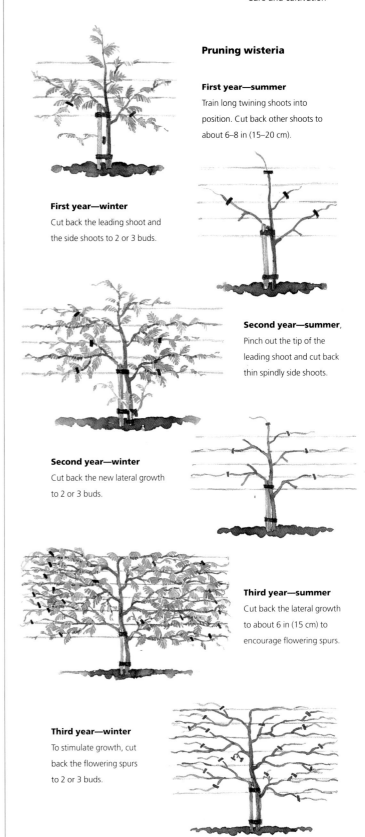

Pruning wisteria

First year—summer
Train long twining shoots into position. Cut back other shoots to about 6–8 in (15–20 cm).

First year—winter
Cut back the leading shoot and the side shoots to 2 or 3 buds.

Second year—summer,
Pinch out the tip of the leading shoot and cut back thin spindly side shoots.

Second year—winter
Cut back the new lateral growth to 2 or 3 buds.

Third year—summer
Cut back the lateral growth to about 6 in (15 cm) to encourage flowering spurs.

Third year—winter
To stimulate growth, cut back the flowering spurs to 2 or 3 buds.

Picture credits

The publishers would like to thank the photographers and garden owners for allowing them to reproduce the photographs on the following pages:

Endpapers M. Harpur; 1 J. Harpur; 2 J. Harpur; 3 J. Harpur; 4–5 J. Harpur; 6–7 J. Harpur/Bodiam Nursery, RHS Show; 8 left J. Harpur/design: Tessa King-Farlow, Birmingham; 8 right M. Harpur/Dr & Mrs Stalbow, Stanmore, Middx; 9 left J. Harpur; 9 right: J. Harpur/Kiftsgate Court, Gloucestershire; 10 J. Harpur; 11 M. Harpur/Royal National Rose Society, St. Albans, Herts; 12 left J. Harpur/ Springfield Gardens, Spalding, Lincolnshire; 12 right J. Harpur/Rodmarton Manor, Gloucestershire; 13 left Andrew Lawson; 13 right J. Harpur; 14 left Justyn Willsmore/Sir Harold Hillier Gardens and Arboretum; 14 right Justyn Willsmore/ Sir Harold Hillier Gardens and Arboretum; 14–15 J. Harpur/ Bradenham Hall, Norfolk; 15 J. Harpur/Home Farm, Balscote, Oxfordshire; 16 M. Harpur; 16–17 M. Harpur/design: Timothy Leese for Mr & Mrs Colin McKay, Norfolk; 18 left J. Harpur/Royal National Rose Society, St. Albans, Herts; 18 right M. Harpur/Royal National Rose Society, St. Albans, Herts; 19 left M. Harpur/ Kypp Cottage, Kent; 19 right J. Harpur/RHS Wisley, Surrey; 19 below J. Harpur/ Royal National Rose Society, St. Albans, Herts; 20 left J. Harpur/ Writtle College, Nr. Chelmsford, Essex; 20 right Andrew Lawson; 21 left J. Harpur/Old Rectory, Sudborough, Northants; 21 right J. Harpur/ Secretts, Godalming, Surrey; 22 David Askham/ Garden Picture Library; 23 clockwise from top left: J. Harpur/ Kiftsgate Court, Gloucestershire; J. Harpur; M. Harpur; J. Harpur; Andrew Lawson; 24 J. Harpur;

25 Justyn Willsmore/Sir Harold Hillier Gardens and Arboretum; 26 M. Harpur/ Sheila Chapman, Chelmsford, Essex; 27 J. Harpur/ design: Jean Goldberry, London; 28 left M. Harpur; 28 right J. Harpur/Plantsman Nursery, Okehampton, Devon; 28–29 M. Harpur/design: Jorn Langberg, Stanton, Suffolk; 29 right J. Harpur/Helmingham Hall, Suffolk; 30 left J. Harpur; 30–31 J. Harpur/design: Susan Ryley, Victoria, B. C., Canada; 31 left M. Harpur/ Kypp Cottage, Kent; 31 right J. Harpur; 32 left J. Harpur; 32 right J. Harpur; 33 J. Harpur; 34–35 below J. Harpur/design: Simon Fraser, Hampton, Middx; 34–35 top J. Harpur; 35 Andrew Lawson; 36 left: Anne Hyde/Lower Severalls, Somerset; 36–37 J. Harpur/ design: Helen Yemm, Flimwell, Sussex; 37 left J. Harpur; 37 right J. Harpur/Stone House Cottage, Worcestershire; 38 J. Harpur/RHS Wisley, Surrey; 39 clockwise from top left: J. Harpur/Saling Hall, Essex; M. Harpur; M. Harpur; M. Harpur; J. Harpur/ Plantsman Nursery, Okehampton, Devon;J. Harpur/RHS Wisley, Surrey; 40 J. Harpur; 41 M. Harpur; 42 left J. Harpur/Beth Chatto Gardens, Essex; 42 right M. Harpur; 43 left M. Harpur/Royal National Rose Society, St. Albans, Herts; 43 right J. Harpur/ Susan Ryley, Victoria, B.C., Canada; 43 below J. Harpur; 44 top left J. Harpur; 44 top right J. Harpur; 44 centre left J. Harpur; 44 centre right J. Harpur; 44 below J. Harpur; 45 J. Harpur; 46 Clive Nichols/Red Gables, Worcestershire; 47 left J. Harper/Royal National Rose Society, St. Albans, Herts; 47 right J. Harpur/ Royal National Rose Society, St. Albans, Herts; 48 left M. Harpur/Plantsman Nursery, Okehampton, Devon; 48 right J. Harpur; 48–49 J. Harpur; 50 J. Harpur; 50–51 M. Harpur; 51 left M. Harpur; 51 right J. Harpur/

Wollerton Old Hall, Shropshire; 52 top Andrew Lawson; 52–53 Anne Hyde/Mrs Ferguson, Maspin House, Hillam, Yorkshire; 53 Howard Rice/Garden Picture Library; 54 left M. Harpur; 54 right J. Harpur/Parc Bagatelle, Paris; 54 below J. Harpur/design: Dan Hinkley, Seattle; 55 J. Harpur/Villa Roquebrune, nr. Cannes, France; 56 left J. Harpur; 56 right J. Harpur; 57 top J. Harpur; 57 below Andrew Lawson; 58 Sunniva Harte/Garden Picture Library/ Little Hutchings, Etchingham, Sussex; 59 top Mayer/Le Scanff/ Garden Picture Library/Jardin de Talos, France; 59 below left Photos Horticultural; 59 below centre Howard Rice/Garden Picture Library/Royal National Rose Society, St. Albans, Herts; 59 below right David Askham/Garden Picture Library; 60 Anne Hyde/Royal National Rose Society, St. Albans, Herts; 61 clockwise from top left: M. Harpur; J. Harpur; M. Harpur; J. Harpur/Writtle College, nr. Chelmsford, Essex; J. Harpur/ Dr & Mrs Grey-Wilson, Suffolk; M. Harpur; 62 J. Harpur/Philippe Levrat, Hyeres, France; 63 M. Harpur; 64 J. S. Sira/Garden Picture Library; 64–65 J. Harpur/ Philippe Levrat, Hyeres, France; 65 M. Harpur; 66 left Howard Rice/ Garden Picture Library; 66 right John Glover/ Garden Picture Library; 67 left Andrew Lawson; 67 right Andrew Lawson; 68 top left Howard Rice/Garden Picture Library; 68 below left Justyn Willsmore/ RHS Wisley, Surrey; 68 centre right Irene Windridge/A–Z Botanical; 69 Andrew Lawson; 70 Howard Rice/ Garden Picture Library; 71 clockwise from top left: M. Harpur; Howard Rice/ Garden Picture Library; Howard Rice/Garden Picture Library; M. Harpur; Andrew Lawson; J. Harpur/Simone de Chazal, Funchal, Madeira; 72–73 J. Harpur; 80 J. Harpur.